teach® yourself

spanish
grammar
juan kattán-ibarra

For over 60 years, more than 40 million people have learnt over 750 subjects the **teach yourself** way, with impressive results.

be where you want to be
with **teach yourself**

The publisher has used its best endeavours to ensure that the URLs for external websites referred to in this book are correct and active at the time of going to press. However, the publisher has no responsibility for the websites and can make no guarantee that a site will remain live or that the content is or will remain appropriate.

For UK order enquiries: please contact Bookpoint Ltd, 130 Milton Park, Abingdon, Oxon OX14 4SB. Telephone: +44 (0) 1235 827720. Fax: +44 (0) 1235 400454. Lines are open 09.00–18.00, Monday to Saturday, with a 24-hour message answering service. Details about our titles and how to order are available at www.teachyourself.co.uk

For USA order enquiries: please contact McGraw-Hill Customer Services, PO Box 545, Blacklick, OH 43004-0545, USA. Telephone: 1-800-722-4726. Fax: 1-614-755-5645.

For Canada order enquiries: please contact McGraw-Hill Ryerson Ltd, 300 Water St, Whitby, Ontario L1N 9B6, Canada. Telephone: 905 430 5000. Fax: 905 430 5020.

Long renowned as the authoritative source for self-guided learning – with more than 40 million copies sold worldwide – the **teach yourself** series includes over 300 titles in the fields of languages, crafts, hobbies, business, computing and education.

British Library Cataloguing in Publication Data: a catalogue record for this title is available from the British Library.

Library of Congress Catalog Card Number: on file.

First published in UK 2000 by Hodder Education, 338 Euston Road, London, NW1 3BH.

First published in US 2000 by Contemporary Books, a division of The McGraw-Hill Companies, 1 Prudential Plaza, 130 East Randolph Street, Chicago, Illinois 60601 USA.

This edition published 2003.

The **teach yourself** name is a registered trade mark of Hodder Headline.

Typeset by Transet Limited, Coventry, England.
Printed in Great Britain for Hodder Education, a division of Hodder Headline, 338 Euston Road, London NW1 3BH, by Cox & Wyman Ltd, Reading, Berkshire.

Hodder Headline's policy is to use papers that are natural, renewable and recyclable products and made from wood grown in sustainable forests. The logging and manufacturing processes are expected to conform to the environmental regulations of the country of origin.

Impression number   10 9 8
Year   2009 2008 2007 2006

contents

About the author

Juan Kattán-Ibarra was born in Chile and lived in Spain for some years. He has degrees in foreign language teaching from the University of Chile, Michigan State University, Manchester University, and the Institute of Education, London University. He taught Spanish at Ealing College and Shell International, and was an examiner in Spanish for the University of London School Examinations Board and the London Chamber of Commerce and Industry. He is now a full-time author.

He is the sole author of *Teach Yourself Spanish*, *Teach Yourself Spanish Extra!*, *Teach Yourself Latin American Spanish*, *Conversational Spanish*, *Conversando*, *Panorama de la prensa*, *Perspectivas culturales de España*, *Perspectivas culturales de Hispanoamérica*, and co-author of *Working with Spanish*, *Talking Business Spanish*, *Se escribe así*, *España nuevo siglo*, *Sueños – World Spanish 2*, *Modern Spanish Grammar*, *Modern Spanish Grammar Workbook* and *Spanish Grammar in Context*.

introduction

This book is designed as a reference guide for those who, with or without the help of a teacher, need to study or revise all the essentials of Spanish grammar. It will also be useful as a companion to your Spanish course. A particular feature of the book is its two-fold approach to the language, from a communicative perspective as well as from a purely grammatical one.

This reference guide covers all the basic language uses, such as *asking and giving personal information, expressing possession, likes and dislikes, obligation and need*, etc. Each one of these language functions leads to the study of the grammatical constructions needed to express it. Important points not covered in the units, as well as some which need special attention are treated separately in the **Grammar reference** section on pages 177–202.

On the contents page, each unit lists both language uses and grammatical terms. This allows you to approach the book from either perspective. If you want to look up a particular grammar point you should consult the index at the back of the book. Grammatical terms with which you may not be familiar are explained in the **Glossary** of grammatical terms starting on page 175.

How to use this book

The following procedure is suggested for working through each unit:

Read the section headed **In this unit you will learn...**, which gives information about the language uses that are studied in the unit, for example how to *say who you are* and *state your nationality*, among other language functions in Unit 1. Then read the **Language points**, which lists the constructions associated with those language uses, for example *subject pronouns* and *present tense* of **ser**, *to be*, in Unit 1. You can then study the **Key sentences** and their English translation, which are intended to ease your way into the **Grammar summary** which follows. The language content of the unit is explained here in terms which you should find easy to follow, each point illustrated by means of further examples, all with their English translation. The vocabulary has been kept simple, so that you can focus your attention on the grammar rather than on the meanings of single words. Try fixing the new language constructions in your memory by writing further examples of your own. Use the **Spanish–English vocabulary**, starting on page 216, and the **English–Spanish vocabulary**, on page 223, to find new words to adapt the sentences in the unit.

Language always functions within a context, so the purpose of the **In context** section, which follows the **Grammar summary**, is to show you how the grammar you have learned in the unit can be used. Read the dialogues and other texts here, paying special attention to the points highlighted in earlier parts of the unit. Key words are listed under each dialogue or text.

To help you consolidate what you have learned, the unit ends with a **Practice** section, containing exercises both grammatical and communicative in nature, which serve as a form of self-assessment. Go through these without looking at the preceding notes, checking your answers in the **Key to the exercises** if necessary. If most or all of your answers are right, and you feel confident with the new language, proceed to the next unit in a similar way. But if you still feel uncertain, go back through the unit again. You may also wish to expand on what you have learned, in which case consult the **Taking it further** section on page 207, where you will find references to other grammar books as well as other useful information related to Spanish, such as websites, language courses and organizations.

Although most words used throughout the units are listed in the **Spanish–English vocabulary** and **English–Spanish vocabulary** at the end of the book, a small pocket dictionary should help you with those which are not, and will also be useful when building up sentences or texts of your own.

01

asking for and giving personal information

In this unit you will learn how to
- say who you are
- state your nationality
- say where you are from
- say what your occupation is
- give similar information about other people
- ask for personal information

Language points
- subject pronouns
- *ser* in the present tense
- gender of nouns
- plural of nouns
- adjectives indicating nationality
- interrogative sentences
- negative sentences

Key sentences

The key sentences and grammar notes which follow will show you how to ask and give simple personal information in Spanish. Look at the sentences and their English translation first then read the **Grammar summary** for an explanation of how the language works.

Saying who you are

Soy Antonio/Ana   *I'm Antonio/Ana*

Stating your nationality

Soy español/española   *I'm Spanish* (man/woman)

Saying where you are from

Soy de Madrid/Salamanca   *I'm from Madrid/Salamanca*

Saying what your occupation is

Soy arquitecto/estudiante   *I'm an architect/student*

Giving similar information about other people

Él es Luis/chileno/profesor   *He's Luis/Chilean/a teacher*
Ella es de Barcelona/Londres *She's from Barcelona/London*

Asking for personal information

¿Es usted Gloria?   *Are you Gloria?* (formal)
Usted es española, ¿no?   *You are Spanish, aren't you?*
                                           (formal/fem.)
¿Eres inglés o americano?   *Are you English or American?*
                                           (informal/masc.)
No eres de aquí, ¿verdad?   *You're not from here, are*
                                           you? (informal)

Grammar summary

1 Subject pronouns

To say *I*, *you*, *he*, *she*, etc. in Spanish, we use the following set of words:

	Singular
yo	*I*
tú	*you* (familiar)
usted	*you* (polite)
él	*he*
ella	*she*
	Plural
nosotros/as	*we* (masc./fem.)
vosotros/as	*you* (familiar, masc./fem.)
ustedes	*you* (polite)
ellos	*they* (masc.)
ellas	*they* (fem.)

Familiar and polite forms of address

Notice that Spanish uses familiar and polite forms of address. The familiar forms (**tú** and **vosotros**) are used very extensively in Spain today, even among people who have never met before. However, in business and official situations, it may generally be safer to use the polite form to start with and then wait and see what the other person is using and do likewise. In writing, **usted** and **ustedes** are normally found in abbreviated form as **Vd.** and **Vds.** or as **Ud.** and **Uds.**

Latin American usage

Latin Americans do not use the familiar plural **vosotros**. Instead, they will use **ustedes**, without differentiating between familiarity and formality. Consequently, the verb forms to address a group of people will be those corresponding to **ustedes**. In the singular, the distinction between **tú** and **usted** still remains.

Omission of subject pronouns

Generally, subject pronouns are omitted in Spanish, except at the start of a conversation, to add emphasis or to avoid ambiguity, as with **él, ella, usted** (and their plural equivalents) which always share the same verb forms.

Él es español	*He's Spanish*
Ella es española	*She's Spanish*
Usted es español	*You're Spanish*

2 *Ser* (to be)

Ser is the verb most frequently used in Spanish when giving basic personal information such as your name, nationality, place of origin and occupation. Here is **ser** fully conjugated in the present tense:

	Singular
yo soy	*I am*
tú eres	*you are* (familiar)
usted es	*you are* (polite)
él, ella es	*he, she is*
	Plural
nosotros/as somos	*we are* (masc./fem.)
vosotros/as sois	*you are* (familiar, masc./fem.)
ustedes son	*you are* (polite)
ellos, ellas son	*they are* (masc./fem.)

For other uses of **ser** see Units 2, 3, 5, 6, 11, and page 200 of the **Grammar reference**.

3 Gender of nouns

Masculine or feminine?

All nouns in Spanish are either masculine or feminine. Nouns which refer to people, such as those indicating professions or occupations, will normally agree in gender with the person referred to. The following simple rules will help you to form the feminine of nouns denoting professions:

- Change the -o to -a.

Él es abogado	*He's a lawyer*
Ella es abogada	*She's a lawyer*

- Add -a to the consonant.

Juan es profesor	*Juan is a teacher*
María es profesora	*María is a teacher*

- Nouns which end in -e do not normally change for masculine and feminine.

Pedro es estudiante	*Pedro is a student*
Carmen es estudiante	*Carmen is a student*

  But there are exceptions:

Él es dependiente	*He's a shop assistant*
Ella es dependienta	*She's a shop assistant*
Él es jefe de ventas	*He's a sales manager*
Ella es jefa de ventas	*She's a sales manager*

- Nouns which end in -ista never change for masculine and feminine.

    Él/Ella es dentista   *He's/She's a dentist*

With certain professions, you may still hear the masculine form used with reference to women, for example:

    Él/Ella es médico   *He's/She's a doctor*

However, new attitudes towards women in Spanish society are bringing about changes in this area of language usage.

There is more on the gender of nouns in Unit 2 and on page 178 of the **Grammar reference**.

4 Plural of nouns

As in English, nouns in Spanish can have singular and plural forms. The plural of nouns is normally formed by adding -s to the singular form, unless the word ends in a consonant, in which case you add -es.

Él es arquitecto	*He's an architect*
Ellos son arquitectos	*They're architects*
Soy doctor	*I'm a doctor*
Somos doctores	*We're doctors*

See also page 179 of the **Grammar reference**.

5 Adjectives indicating nationality

Masculine or feminine?

Adjectives of nationality, like many adjectives in Spanish, have masculine and feminine forms. To form the feminine from a masculine adjective of nationality or origin, change -o to -a or add -a to the consonant, as in:

John es británico	*John is British*
Sarah es británica	*Sarah is British*
Peter es inglés	*Peter is English*
Ann es inglesa	*Ann is English*

Singular and plural

The plural of adjectives, like that of nouns, is normally formed by adding -s to the singular form, unless the word ends in a consonant, in which case you add -es.

John es británico	*John is British*
John y Sarah son británicos	*John and Sarah are British*
Peter es inglés	*Peter is English*
Peter y Ann son ingleses	*Peter and Ann are English*

Notice that when the adjective refers to both male and female the masculine form is used.

Adjectives which end in **-i** and **-ú** add **-es** to form the plural.

Él es paquistaní	*He's Pakistani*
Ellos son paquistaníes	*They're Pakistani*
Ella es hindú	*She's Indian*
Ellas son hindúes	*They're Indian*

Adjectives which end in **-z** change **-z** into **-c** and add **-es**.

Paco es andaluz	*Paco is Andalusian*
Paco y Antonio son andaluces	*Paco and Antonio are Andalusian*

6 Interrogative sentences

It is possible to form questions in Spanish in several ways:

* Using the same word order as in a statement, but with a rising intonation.

    ¿Usted es española?   *Are you Spanish?*

* Reversing the order subject–verb.

    ¿Es usted irlandés?   *Are you Irish?*

* Using either **¿verdad?** (literally, *true*) or **¿no?** attached to the statement.

    Usted es escocés, **¿verdad?** *You're Scottish, aren't you?*
    Ella es americana, **¿no?** *She's American, isn't she?*

7 Negative sentences

Negative sentences are formed simply by using the word **no** before the verb.

¿**No** es usted español?   *Aren't you Spanish?*
No, **no** soy español   *No, I'm not Spanish*

Notice the double negative, as in English, in the second sentence.

8 Asking for and giving information about marital status

To ask for and give information about marital status use the verb **estar** also meaning *to be*. **Estar** is normally used when referring to states or conditions, such as the state of being single or married. (See Unit 3.)

| ¿Está soltero/a o casado/a? | *Is he/she single or married?* |
| Está soltera | *She's single* |

Latin Americans usually use **ser** in this context.

| Carlos es casado | *Carlos is married* |

In context

1 Study these conversations between people who just met and are getting to know each other. The first exchange is formal and the second one informal.

a	**Señor**	¿Es Vd. española?
	Señora	Sí, soy española, ¿y Vd.?
	Señor	Soy mexicano. Soy de Guadalajara.
	Señora	Yo soy de Madrid.

| **sí** | *yes* |
| **y** | *and* |

b	**Carlos**	Hola. ¿Cómo te llamas?
	Carmen	Me llamo Carmen, ¿y tú?
	Carlos	Yo soy Carlos López. ¿Eres de Madrid?
	Carmen	No, no soy de Madrid. Soy de Salamanca.

| **hola** | *hello* |
| **¿cómo te llamas?** | *what's your name?* (fam.) |

2 Look at this piece of writing which gives personal information.

*Me llamo Alfonso González, soy
español, de Sevilla. Soy estudiante
de medicina ...*

To ask someone's name in a formal way use the phrase:

¿Cómo se llama Vd.?	*What's your name?*
	(literally, *what are you*
	called?)

When giving your occupation or profession Spanish does not use the equivalent of the English word *a*, e.g. **Soy profesor**, *I'm a teacher*.

Practice

1 You are writing to a Spanish-speaking correspondent for the first time. Try putting the following information in Spanish.

a Say what your name is.
b Say your nationality.
c Say what town or city you are from.
d Say what your occupation is.
e Say whether you are single or married.

2 At a party you are introduced to someone who only speaks Spanish. Can you fill in your questions in this dialogue?

– Hola, ¿...?
– Me llamo Antonio.
– ¿...?
– No, no soy español. Soy argentino.
– ¿...?
– Sí, soy de Buenos Aires.
– ¿...?
– Sí, soy estudiante. Estudio inglés y alemán.

3 What do these people do for a living? Match the names with the occupations listed below and write sentences saying what they do. Use the appropriate gender in each case.

| médico/a estudiante taxista |
| mecánico/a peluquero/a camarero/a (mesero/a, L. Am.) |

a Antonio Morales

b Silvia Pérez

c Alfredo Muñoz

d Juan González

e Javier Díaz

f Francisco Mella

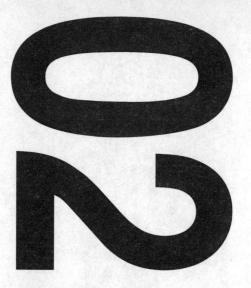

02

identifying people, places and things

In this unit you will learn how to
- introduce people
- greet people when being introduced
- identify people, places and things
- ask questions in order to identify people, places and things

Language points
- demonstrative adjectives and pronouns
- *ser* in introductions and identifications
- definite articles
- interrogative words *¿quién?, ¿cuál?, ¿qué?*
- possessive adjective *mi*

Key sentences

To introduce people, and to identify people, places and things you can use the Spanish equivalent of words such as *this*, *that*, *these*, *those*.

Questions leading to identification, for example *Who's that man?*, *What's that?* require the use of interrogative words.

The key sentences and grammar notes which follow will show you how to express these ideas in Spanish.

Introducing people

Ésta es Carmen/mi mujer	*This is Carmen/my wife*
Éste es Raúl/mi hermano	*This is Raúl/my brother*

Greeting people when being introduced

Encantado/a	*Pleased to meet you (man/woman)*
Mucho gusto	*Pleased to meet you*
Hola	*Hello*

Identifying people, places and things

Ésa es la señora Ruiz/mi casa	*That's señora Ruiz/my house*
Ésos son mis amigos/libros	*Those are my friends/books*
Aquélla es la montaña	*That's the mountain*

Asking questions leading to the identification of people, places and things

¿Quién es ese señor/esa señora?	*Who's that gentleman/lady?*
¿Cuál es tu oficina/habitación?	*Which is your office/room?*
¿Qué es esto/eso?	*What's this/that?*

Grammar summary

1 Demonstrative adjectives and pronouns

Look at the preceding examples once again and study the Spanish equivalent of *this*, *these* and *that*, *those*. Unlike English, which only distinguishes between singular and plural, Spanish also makes a distinction between masculine and feminine.

Forms of demonstratives

This, these (next to you)

este señor (masc.)	*this gentleman*
esta señora (fem.)	*this lady*
estos señores (masc.)	*these gentlemen*
estas señoras (fem.)	*these ladies*

That, those (near you)

ese hotel (masc.)	*that hotel*
esa habitación (fem.)	*that room*
esos hoteles (masc.)	*those hotels*
esas habitaciones (fem.)	*those rooms*

Spanish also differs from English in having a separate set of words to identify or point at someone or something which is far from you. In English, however, the translation would still be *that, those*.

aquel chico (masc.)	*that boy*
aquella chica (fem.)	*that girl*
aquellos chicos (masc.)	*those boys*
aquellas chicas (fem.)	*those girls*

Adjectives and pronouns

In all the previous examples, the demonstratives have been followed by nouns (e.g. **este señor, ese hotel, aquel chico**), in which case words such as **este, ese, aquel** are functioning as adjectives. But they may also be used to refer to a noun without mentioning it specifically, for example **éste** (*this one*), **ése** (*that one*), **aquél** (*that one*). In this case, they act as pronouns, and they are normally written with an accent, to distinguish them from the adjectives.

Neuter demonstratives

Neuter forms are used when we are not referring to a specific noun, as in:

¿Qué es **esto**?	*What's this?*
¿Qué es **eso**?	*What's that?*
¿Qué es **aquello**?	*What's that?*
Quiero **esto/eso**	*I want this/that*

2 *Ser* in introductions and identification

Notice the use of **ser** – **es** for singular and **son** for plural – for identifying people, places and things:

Ése es el señor García	*That is Mr García*
Éste es mi pueblo	*This is my town*
Aquéllas son mis llaves	*Those are my keys*

If we are introducing or identifying ourselves we need to use **soy** in the singular and **somos** in the plural, for example:

| **Soy** Paco Martínez | *I'm Paco Martínez* |
| **Somos** los señores García | *We're the Garcías* |

Notice also the use of **ser** when enquiring about someone or something:

| ¿Quién **es** esa señorita? | *Who's that young lady?* |
| ¿Cuál **es** el coche? | *Which is the car?* |

For the full forms of **ser** see Unit 1.

3 Definite articles (*the*)

As we saw in Unit 1, all nouns in Spanish are either masculine or feminine and, as in English, there are singular and plural forms. Likewise, the definite article (*the*) has different forms depending on the gender (masculine or feminine) and number (singular or plural) of the noun it qualifies:

el hotel (masc. sing.)	*the hotel*
la habitación (fem. sing.)	*the room*
los hoteles (masc. pl.)	*the hotels*
las habitaciones (fem. pl.)	*the rooms*

But before a feminine noun beginning with a stressed **a-** or **ha-** we must use **el** and not **la**.

el agua	*water*
el arte	*art*
el hambre	*hunger*

The noun, however, is still feminine. Notice:

el agua fría	*cold water*
las aguas	*waters*
las artes plásticas	*plastic arts*

There is more on the use of the definite article on pages 177–8 of the **Grammar reference**.

4 Interrogative words *quién, cuál, qué*

To ask questions in order to identify people, places and things we may need words such as **¿quién?** (*who?*), **¿cuál?** (*which?, what?*) and **¿qué?** (*what?*).

Quién – quiénes

Quién translates into English as *who*:

¿Quién es aquel muchacho?   *Who's that boy?*
¿Quién es aquella muchacha? *Who's that girl?*

If we are referring to more than one person we must use the plural form **quiénes** followed by the plural form of the verb:

¿Quiénes son esas personas? *Who are those people?*
¿Quiénes son esos niños?   *Who are those children?*

Cuál – cuáles

The most usual translation of **cuál** into English is *which*, as in:

¿Cuál es la maleta?   *Which is the suitcase?*
¿Cuál es el equipaje? *Which is the luggage?*

The Spanish equivalent of *which are ...?* is ¿**cuáles son ...?**, as in:

¿Cuáles son los billetes? *Which are the tickets?*
¿Cuáles son las cartas?   *Which are the letters?*

Notice also the use of **cuál – cuáles** in sentences where English would normally require the use of *what*:

¿Cuál es el problema?   *What's the problem?*
¿Cuáles son las ventajas? *What are the advantages?*

Remember

The English construction *what* + *to be* + *noun* normally translates into Spanish as ¿**cuál es ...?**, ¿**cuáles son ...?**

Qué

Qué translates normally as *what*, for example:

¿Qué es eso?   *What's that?*
¿Qué es esto? *What's this?*

But when it functions as an adjective, it sometimes translates as *which*:

¿Qué libro es?   *Which book is it?*
¿Qué habitación es? *Which room is it?*

Notice the use of the accent in all interrogative words: ¿quién?, ¿cuál?, ¿qué?, etc.

5 Possessive adjective *mi*

The Spanish equivalent of *my* as in *my friend*, varies in number depending on whether the noun which follows is singular or plural, but there is no variation for masculine or feminine:

Ésa es **mi** amiga Isabel   *That is my friend Isabel*
Éstos son **mis** amigos   *These are my Chilean friends*
    chilenos

For the full forms and usage of possessive adjectives and pronouns see Unit 6.

6 Other ways of introducing people

Here are some alternative ways of introducing people:

Informal

Te presento a Juan   *May I introduce Juan?*
¿Conoces a Ana?   *Do you know/Have you met*
                            Ana?

Formal

Le presento a María   *May I introduce María?*
¿Conoce Vd. a Isabel?   *Do you know/Have you met*
                            Isabel?

In context

1 Study these conversations in which people are being introduced. The first exchange is informal and the second one formal.

a Cristina ¿Qué tal Isabel?
Isabel   Hola Cristina, ¿cómo estás?
Cristina Bien, gracias. Ésta es Gloria, mi amiga argentina.
Isabel   Hola.
Gloria   Hola.

¿qué tal?	*how are you?* (informal)
¿cómo estás?	*how are you?* (informal)
bien, gracias	*fine, thank you*

b Señora Gómez Buenas tardes, señor Ramos. ¿Cómo está Vd.?
Señor Ramos   Muy bien, ¿y Vd.?
Señora Gómez Bien, gracias. Éste es José, mi marido.
Señor Ramos   Mucho gusto, señor.
Señor Gómez   Encantado.

¿cómo está Vd.?	*how are you?* (formal)
muy bien	*very well*

2 Getting to know people

Rodolfo	¿Quién es aquella chica?
Alvaro	¿Cuál?
Rodolfo	Aquella chica de azul.
Alvaro	Ésa es Marta. Es guapa, ¿eh?

de azul	*in blue*
guapo/a	*pretty, good looking*

Rodolfo	Sí, muy guapa.

Practice

1 Fill in the gaps in these sentences with suitable interrogative words. Choose from the following: **¿qué?, ¿cuál/cuáles?, ¿quién/quiénes?**

a ¿... es ese señor?
b ¿... es la idea?
c ¿... son esos chicos?
d ¿... es esto?
e ¿... es tu habitación?
f ¿... son las maletas?

2 Carmen is introducing her family to some friends. Fill in the gaps in the dialogue with suitable words and phrases.

Carmen	Hola José, ¿...?
José	Bien, gracias.
Carmen	Te ... a mi familia. ... es Juan, mi marido.
José	Mucho ...
Juan	Encantado.
Carmen	... es Julia, mi hermana, y ... son mis hijos Pablo y Luis.

03

describing people, places and things

In this unit you will learn how to
- describe people, places and things
- describe the weather
- ask what someone or something is like

Language points
- *ser* in description
- *estar* in description
- adjectives
- interrogative word *cómo*
- *hacer* in description of the weather
- *tener* in description

Key sentences

The key sentences and grammar notes which follow will show
you how to use **ser** and **estar** (*to be*) in the description of people,
places and things. You will also learn to talk about the weather
using a construction with **hacer** (literally *to do, make*).

Describing people, places and things

Roberto es alto/simpático	*Roberto is tall/nice*
Las playas son buenas/limpias	*The beaches are good/clean*
La comida es excelente/ abundante	*The food is excellent /plentiful*

Describing people, places and things at a point in time

Está muy guapa/elegante	*She looks very pretty/elegant*
La ciudad está sucia/fea	*The city looks dirty/ugly*
Esta leche/carne no está buena	*This milk/meat is off*

Describing the weather

Hace (mucho/un poco de) frío/calor	*It's (very/a little) cold/warm*

Asking what someone or something is like

¿Cómo es el personal/hotel?	*What's the staff/hotel like?*
¿Cómo es el tiempo/clima?	*What the weather/climate like?*

Grammar summary

1 *Ser* and *estar* (to be)

There are two ways of saying *to be* in Spanish – **ser** and **estar** –
and the uses of each are clearly differentiated by the native
speaker, as you will see from the explanations and examples that
follow. See also pages 200–1 of the **Grammar reference**.

2 *Ser* used in description

Ser is the verb most frequently used in description. In this
context, it is generally used with adjectives which refer to:

a Characteristics which are considered as permanent, e.g. physical and mental characteristics:

Víctor **es** delgado	*Victor is thin*
Mercedes **es** inteligente	*Mercedes is intelligent*

b Characteristics which, although subjective, may be considered as true by the speaker:

El español **es** fácil	*Spanish is easy*
El árabe **es** difícil	*Arabic is difficult*

c Characteristics which are considered as universal:

La Tierra **es** redonda	*The earth is round*
El oro **es** un metal	*Gold is a metal*

d Certain states or conditions such as **inocente** (*innocent*), **culpable** (*guilty*), **pobre** (*poor*), **feliz** (*happy*), **desgraciado** (*unhappy*):

Ella **es** inocente	*She's innocent*
Ellos **son** felices	*They're happy*
Son países pobres	*They're poor countries*

For other uses of **ser** see Units 5, 6, 11 and page 200 of the **Grammar reference**.

3 *Estar* used in description

Estar is not normally used in description, except with adjectives which refer to a state or condition, for example:

Cecilia **está** triste	*Cecilia is (looks) sad*
Ricardo **está** contento	*Ricardo is happy*

Some adjectives may be used with either **ser** or **estar**. **Ser** refers to the nature of what is being described while **estar** denotes a state or condition at a particular point in time. Consider these sentences:

Jorge **es** elegante	*Jorge is elegant* (always)
Jorge **está** elegante	*Jorge is (looks) elegant* (now)
Mónica **es** gorda	*Mónica is fat* (general characteristic)
Mónica **está** gorda	*Mónica is fat* (now)

It is not correct to say – as some textbooks do – that **ser** always refers to permanent characteristics while **estar** refers to states which are transitory. The following examples defeat that rule:

Mi madre **está** muerta   *My mother is dead*
Cádiz **está** en Andalucía   *Cádiz is in Andalusia*

Present tense of *estar*

Here is **estar** fully conjugated in the present tense:

	Singular		Plural
estoy	*I am*	estamos	*we are*
estás	*you are* (fam.)	estáis	*you are* (fam.)
está	*you are* (pol.)	están	*you are* (pol.)
	he/she/it is		*they are*

For other uses of **estar** see Units 5 and 8 and page 201 of the
Grammar reference.

4 Adjectives

To be able to describe things you need adjectives. In Spanish we
can distinguish the following types of adjectives.

• Adjectives which agree in number and gender with the noun

Most Spanish adjectives fall in this category, and within this
group we have most of those ending in -o, for example **bajo**,
short. Adjectives ending in -or, for example **trabajador**,
hardworking, also fall in this group.

These adjectives form the feminine by changing -o into -a (e.g.
pequeño, **pequeña**, *small*) or by adding -a to the consonant (e.g.
encantador, **encantadora**, *enchanting*). The plural is formed by
adding -s to the vowel (e.g. **pequeños**) or -es to the consonant
(e.g. **encantadores**).

• Adjectives which agree only in number

Within this group are included most adjectives ending in a
consonant, for example **fácil**, *easy*, **azul**, *blue*, **feliz**, *happy*.
Other adjectives in this category are those ending in -a (e.g.
hipócrita, *hypocritical*) and -e (e.g. **grande**, *big*).

To form the plural add -s to the final vowel (e.g. **grande**,
grandes) or -es to the consonant (e.g. **fácil**, **fáciles**). But if the
word ends in -z, change the -z to -c and then add -es (e.g. **feliz**,
felices).

• Adjectives which are invariable

A few adjectives do not change for number or gender. Among these we find loan words from other languages, for example **beige** as well as some adjectives describing colour, especially those which may also function as nouns. Examples of these are **naranja** (*orange*), **violeta** (*violet*) and **rosa** (*pink, rose*).

Agreement of adjectives

As a general rule, in the presence of one or more than one masculine noun, use the masculine form of the adjective, e.g. **libros y periódicos españoles**, *Spanish books and newspapers*.

In the presence of one or more feminine nouns, use the feminine form of the adjective, e.g. **escuelas y universidades americanas**, *American schools and universities*.

If there are nouns of different gender you will need to use the masculine form of the adjective, e.g. **hombres y mujeres mexicanos** *Mexican men and women*.

Short forms

A few adjectives have short forms: **grande** (*large, big*) shortens to **gran** before a masculine or feminine singular noun:

un coche **grande**	*a big car*
un **gran** coche	*a big car*
una ciudad **grande**	*a big city*
una **gran** ciudad	*a big city*

When **grande** precedes the noun it often translates into English as *great*:

un **gran** hombre	*a great man*
una **gran** mentira	*a great lie*

Bueno (*good*) and **malo** (*bad*) drop the ending **-o** when they come before a masculine noun:

un libro **bueno**	*a good book*
un **buen** libro	*a good book*
un día **malo**	*a bad day*
un **mal** día	*a bad day*

Intensive forms

To intensify the meaning of a descriptive adjective we can add to it the suffix **-ísimo** (masculine) or **-ísima** (feminine). Adjectives which end in a vowel must drop the vowel before adding -ísimo/a. See what happens to **difícil** (*difficult*), **caro** (*expensive*) and **sabroso** (*tasty*):

Es dificilísimo	*It's very difficult*
Es carísimo	*It's very expensive*
La comida está sabrosísima	*The food is very tasty*

Notice the following spelling changes when adding -ísimo/a. Adjectives which end in -co, e.g. **rico** (*rich*) change the **c** to **qu** before adding this suffix:

Él es riquísimo	*He's very rich*

Adjectives which end in **-ble**, e.g. **amable** (*kind*) change **-ble** into **-bil** before adding **ísimo**:

Ella es amabilísima	*She's very kind*

As there are a number of adjectives which cannot take -ísimo/a it is best not to use this suffix if you're not sure. Instead, you can use an intensifier such as **muy** (*very*), **demasiado** (*too*), or **bastante** (*quite*):

Es **muy** barato	*It's very cheap*
Está **demasiado** caliente	*It's too hot*
Él es **bastante** raro	*He's quite strange*

Position of adjectives

Adjectives often follow the noun they describe:

Es un problema **difícil**	*It's a difficult problem*
Es una chica **alta**	*She's a tall girl*

Descriptive adjectives are sometimes placed before the noun to show emphasis, affection or some other desired effect:

Es una **buena** idea	*It's a good idea*
Es una **pequeña** casa	*It's a small house*

For comparison of adjectives see page 181 of the **Grammar reference**.

5 Interrogative word *cómo*

Cómo normally translates into English as *how*, as in questions enquiring about the state or condition of someone or something:

¿**Cómo** está Fernando?	*How's Fernando?*
¿**Cómo** están ellos?	*How are they?*

But in questions asking what someone or something is like, cómo translates into English as *what*:

¿Cómo es Fernando?   *What's Fernando like?*
¿Cómo son ellos?   *What are they like?*

Remember
To enquire about a state or condition we use **estar**, while to ask questions regarding characteristics we must use **ser**.

6 *Hacer* in description of the weather

To describe the weather Spanish normally uses the verb **hacer** (literally, *to do*, *make*) in the 3rd person singular plus a noun.

Hace (mucho) frío   *It's (very) cold*
Hace (demasiado) calor   *It's (too) hot*
Hace (un poco de) viento   *It's (a little) windy*

7 Other ways of describing the weather

Although the weather is normally described with **hacer**, e.g. **hace calor**, *it's warm*, the climate in general may be described with **ser** (*to be*) or **tener** (*to have*):

El clima es (muy)   *The climate is (very) hot/cold*
  caluroso/frío
Tiene un clima húmedo/   *It has a wet/mild climate*
  templado

8 *Tener* in description

Another verb often used in description is **tener**, *to have*: **tiene** (*you have*, *he/she/it has*), **tienen** (*you/they have*):

Ella tiene ojos verdes/   *She has green eyes/*
  el cabello largo   *long hair*
Esta ciudad tiene mucho   *This city has a lot of charm*
  encanto

For the full forms of **tener** see Units 4 and 6.

9 Describing things in terms of the material they are made of

Es de madera/metal   *It's made of wood/metal*
Son de lana/oro   *They're made of wool/gold*

In context

1 Describing someone.

A ¿Quién es ese señor?
B Es el nuevo profesor de español.
A ¿Cómo es?
B Es simpático, pero es muy estricto.
A ¿Es buen profesor?
B Sí, es un profesor excelente.

nuevo	*new*
estricto	*strict*

2 Read this extract from a letter describing a place.

Querido Jorge,

*Ésta es mi primera visita a Cadaqués. Es un lugar precioso
y el hotel es estupendo, aunque es un poco caro. Hace
muchísimo calor ...*

mi primera visita	*my first visit*
un lugar precioso	*a very nice place*
aunque	*although*

Ésta es mi primera visita a Cadaqués. Notice the position of the
ordinal number **primera**. Ordinal numbers normally precede the
noun they qualify.

Practice

1 Can you describe each of the following? Use full sentences
and appropriate adjectives from the list:

elegante	gordo
delgado	bajo
alto	triste
redondo	limpio

2 In a letter to a Spanish-speaking friend you describe a town you are visiting for the first time. Use the following phrases and an appropriate verb from the list to write a paragraph about the place:

> estar   ser   tener   hacer
> una ciudad muy bonita   la gente muy simpática y el clima
> bastante bueno   no demasiado calor   el hotel excelente
> un restaurante muy bueno y dos bares
> también una playa estupenda   (yo) muy contento/a aquí

Now try describing your own town.

04

expressing existence and availability

In this unit you will learn how to
- express existence
- enquire about existence
- express availability
- enquire about availability
- enquire about quantity

Language points
- *hay*
- *tener* in the present tense
- indefinite articles
- interrogative word cuánto
- *alguien* and *nadie*
- *alguno* and *ninguno*
- *algo* and *nada*
- other verbs expressing existence and availability

Key sentences

This unit focuses on the use of **hay**, *there is/are, is/are there?*, for expressing existence, and the use of **tener**, *to have*, to express availability.

Have a look at these key sentences and their English translations before going on to the **Grammar summary**.

Expressing existence

Hay un restaurante/una piscina	*There's a restaurant/ swimming pool*
Hay dos hoteles/tres ascensores	*There are two hotels/three lifts*
No **hay** nada	*There's nothing*

Enquiring about existence

¿**Hay** alguna farmacia/ algún banco por aquí?	*Is there a chemist's/ bank nearby?*
¿**Hay** museos/bibliotecas allí?	*Are there any museums/ libraries there?*

Expressing availability

Tengo/tenemos dos habitaciones disponibles	*I/we have two rooms available*
No **tienen** ningún coche/ ninguna habitación	*They haven't got a (single) car/room*

Enquiring about availability

¿**Tiene/tienen** una mesa/ habitación para dos?	*Have you got a table/ room for two?*
¿**Tenéis** algo para mí?	*Have you got something for me?*

Enquiring about quantity

¿Cuántos coches/cuántas personas **hay**?	*How many cars/people are there?*
¿Cuánto dinero/cuánta comida **hay**?	*How much money/food is there?*

Grammar summary

1 *Hay* (there is/are, is/are there?)

To say *there is/are* and *is/are there?* Spanish uses the single word **hay**. In negative sentences **no** precedes the word **hay**.

¿Hay un hotel por aquí?	*Is there a hotel around here?*
Hay uno/dos	*There is/are one/two*
¿Hay alguno?	*Is there one?*
No hay ninguno	*There isn't (a single) one*

2 *Tener* (to have)

One of several functions of **tener** (*to have*) is the expression of availability. **Tener** is an irregular verb. Its present tense forms are:

Singular		Plural	
tengo	*I have*	tenemos	*we have*
tienes	*you have* (fam.)	tenéis	*you have* (fam.)
tiene	*you have* (pol.)	tienen	*you have* (pol.)
	he/she/it has		*they have*

¿**Tiene** Vd. cambio?	*Have you got any change?*
Lo siento, no **tengo**	*I'm sorry, I haven't*
¿**Tienen** Vds. una habitación individual?	*Have you got a single room?*
Sí, **tenemos**	*Yes, we have*

3 Indefinite articles (a/an)

The word for *a* is **un** for masculine nouns and **una** for feminine nouns.

Masculine

¿Hay **un** supermercado por aquí?	*Is there a supermarket around here?*
Hay **un** restaurante	*There is a restaurant*

Feminine

¿Tienen Vds. **una** habitación?	*Have you got a room?*
¿Tiene Vd. **una** mesa?	*Have you got a table?*

The plural forms **unos, unas** are translated into English as *some*:

unos restaurantes	*some restaurants*
unas habitaciones	*some rooms*

Spanish does not use the equivalent of English *a* when you indicate your own or someone else's occupation. Compare these phrases:

¿Hay un camarero?	*Is there a waiter?*
Paco es camarero	*Paco is a waiter*
Yo soy recepcionista	*I'm a receptionist*

4 Interrogative word *cuánto*

¿Cuánto? agrees in number (singular and plural) and gender (masculine and feminine) with the noun it refers to:

¿Cuánto tiempo tenemos?	*How much time have we got?*
¿Cuánta fruta hay?	*How much fruit is there?*
¿Cuántos invitados hay?	*How many guests are there?*
¿Cuántas personas hay?	*How many people are there?*

¿Cuánto? may replace a noun when this is understood:

¿Cuántos libros hay?	*How many books are there?*
¿Cuántos hay?	*How many are there?*
¿Cuánta gente hay?	*How many people are there?*
¿Cuánta hay?	*How many are there?*

Here are some words and phrases which may be used in reply to the question **¿cuánto/s?**:

Hay mucho(a)/un poco	*There is a lot/a little*
Hay muchos(as)/pocos(as)	*There are many/a few.*
Hay suficiente(s)	*There is/are enough*
Hay bastante(s)	*There is/are plenty*

5 *Alguien* (somebody/someone, anybody/anyone)

Alguien is an invariable pronoun which is used in positive and interrogative sentences:

¿Hay **alguien** allí?	*Is there anyone there?*
Hay **alguien** en la puerta	*There's someone at the door*

6 *Nadie* (nobody/no one)

Nadie is a negative word which may follow the verb, as in:

Allí no hay **nadie**	*There's nobody there*
En la puerta no hay **nadie**	*There's nobody at the door*

Notice that in this construction Spanish must use a double negative.

Nadie may also precede the verb, acting as the subject of a sentence, for example:

Nadie tiene fuego	*No one has a light*
Nadie tiene tiempo	*No one has time*

Notice that in this construction the negative **no** must be omitted.

7 *Alguno* (some/any)

Alguno varies in gender and number according to the noun it modifies (acting as an adjective) or the noun it refers to (acting as a pronoun). Its forms are **algún, alguno, algunos, alguna, algunas.**

Algún

This word is used before a singular masculine noun:

¿Hay **algún** banco por aquí?	*Is there a bank around here?*
¿Hay **algún** museo en la ciudad?	*Is there any museum in the city?*

Alguno/s, alguna/s

Here are some examples of how these words are used:

¿Tiene Vd. **alguno**?	*Have you got any?*
Tenemos **algunos** billetes solamente	*We only have a few tickets*
Ya hay **algunas** personas en la reunión	*There are already some people at the meeting*

In singular sentences **algún, alguno, alguna** may be replaced by **uno/a.**

¿Hay **algún** café por aquí?	*Is there a café around here?*
¿Hay **un** café por aquí?	*Is there a café around here?*

8 *Ninguno* (no/any/none/nobody)

Ninguno is a negative word which normally occurs in the singular as **ningún** (before masculine nouns), **ninguno** or **ninguna.** This negative word may follow the verb, as in:

No hay **ningún** bar	*There isn't a bar*
No hay **ninguno**	*There isn't one/any*
No tenemos **ninguna** reserva	*We have no reservation*
No tenemos **ninguna**	*We don't have one/any*

Notice that in this construction Spanish must use a double negative.

Ninguno may sometimes precede the verb, as in:

Ningún banco tiene cajero automático	*No bank has a cash point*
Ninguno tiene cajero automático	*None of them has a cash point*

9 *Algo* (some/any/something/anything)

Algo is an invariable pronoun which normally follows the verb:

Hay **algo** de dinero	*There some money*
¿Hay **algo** de comer?	*Is there something to eat?*
¿Necesitas **algo**?	*Do you need anything?*

10 *Nada* (nothing/any)

Nada is a negative word which normally follows the verb:

No hay **nada** de carne	*There isn't any meat*
No hay **nada**	*There is nothing*

Notice the double negative in this construction.

11 Other verbs expressing existence and availability

Existence and availability may also be expressed with **existir** (*to exist*), **contar con** (*to have*), and **disponer de** (*to have*). These are overall less frequent than **hay** and **tener**, and tend to be used in more formal contexts:

En Madrid **existen** buenos museos	*In Madrid there are good museums*
¿**Con** cuánto dinero **contamos**?	*How much money do we have?*
No **disponen de** tiempo	*They don't have time*

In context

1 Study this conversation between a tourist and a hotel receptionist.

Recepcionista	Buenos días.
Turista	Buenos días. ¿Tiene alguna habitación?
Recepcionista	¿Para cuántas personas?

| **Turista** | Para dos. |
| **Recepcionista** | Tenemos una interior solamente. Exterior no tenemos ninguna. |

para	*for*
una (habitación) interior	*a room at the back*
una (habitación) exterior	*a room facing the street*

2 Read this text describing the facilities available at a hotel.

El Hotel Don Carlos es un hotel de cuatro estrellas. El hotel tiene cien habitaciones dobles, treinta individuales y cuatro suites. Todas las habitaciones tienen baño privado, teléfono y televisión.

En el Hotel Don Carlos hay tres restaurantes y dos bares. También hay una piscina muy grande y una sauna. El hotel tiene aparcamiento propio para los clientes. Además, hay una sala de convenciones muy cómoda y moderna para trescientas personas.

todos/as	*all*
el baño privado	*private bathroom*
proprio/a	*own*
además	*besides*
una sala de convenciones	*a conference room*

Notice the use of **para** in the following phrases:

¿para cuántas personas?	*for how many people?*
para dos personas	*for two people*
para los clientes	*for the clients*
para 300 personas	*for 300 people*

Practice

1 You have just arrived in a Spanish-speaking town and you want to find out about some of the facilities in and around the hotel where you are staying.

a Ask if the hotel has a restaurant.
b Ask if there is a swimming pool.
c A couple of friends are arriving today, so ask the receptionist if he has a double room.
d Ask if the hotel has a car park.
e Ask if there is a supermarket nearby.
f Ask if there are museums in the town.

2 You are describing your own town and your neighbourhood to a Spanish-speaking acquaintance. Say what places of interest there are and what facilities you can find. Look up new words in your dictionary if necessary. Here is an example:

Ejemplo: **Hay un museo de arte.**

3 You have been visiting friends at the house below, and on your return home you describe this in a letter to a Spanish - speaking friend. Fill in the blanks with **hay** or the correct form of **ser** or **tener**, as appropriate. More than one form may be correct in some cases.

La casa de Laura y José (1) .... muy agradable, y (2) .... una vista (*view*) espectacular. La casa no (3) .... demasiado grande, (4) .... tres habitaciones solamente, pero (5) .... muy cómoda. En el salón (6) .... una biblioteca (*bookshelf*) con algunos libros muy interesantes, y (7) .... un cuadro (*picture*) moderno muy bueno. En el dormitorio (*bedroom*) (ellos) (8) .... una pequeña colección de libros en inglés.

José (9) .... un excelente cocinero (*cook*) y la casa (10) .... una cocina muy bien equipada. Laura prefiere (*to prefer*) el jardín y ella (11) .... un jardín precioso.

La ciudad (12) .... pequeña, pero (13) .... algunos museos muy buenos y una catedral muy bonita. El museo principal (14) .... una buena colección de pintura (*painting*) española.

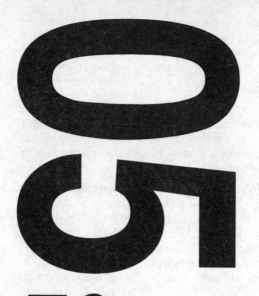

05

expressing location

In this unit you will learn how to
- express location
- express distance
- ask questions regarding location and distance
- ask and answer questions regarding the location of events
- give simple directions

Language points
- *estar* in the expression of location and distance
- Interrogative word *dónde*
- words and phrases used in the expression of location and distance
- *ser* to refer to the location of events
- other verbs denoting location

Key sentences

To say where something or someone is or how far a place is Spanish normally uses the verb **estar,** *to be.*

To say where an event is taking place you need to use **ser,** *to be.*

To learn more about this, look at the key sentences and the grammar notes which follow.

Expressing location

El mercado/banco está allí — *The market/bank is there*
Los teléfonos/servicios están abajo — *The telephones/toilets are downstairs*

Expressing distance

La iglesia está a dos calles/cinco minutos de aquí — *The church is two streets/five minutes from here*

Asking questions regarding location and distance

¿Dónde está la oficina de turismo/cambio? — *Where is the tourist office/bureau de change?*
¿A qué distancia está Burgos/Málaga? — *How far is Burgos/Malaga?*

Asking and answering questions regarding the location of events

¿Dónde es la reunión/la fiesta? — *Where is the meeting/party?*
Es en mi oficina/casa — *It's in my office/house*

Giving simple directions

La plaza está al final de esta calle/a la derecha — *The square is at this end of this street/on the right*
El museo está enfrente/al lado de la catedral — *The museum is opposite/next to the cathedral*

Grammar summary

1 *Estar* in the expression of location and distance

Estar (*to be*) is the verb most frequently used in Spanish when expressing location and distance. It is normally used in the third person singular or plural, followed immediately by a preposition, e.g. **en** (*in, on, at*), **entre** (*between*), or an adverb of place, e.g. **aquí** (*here*), **allí** (*there*), **enfrente** (*opposite*). (For the full forms of **estar** see Unit 3). Examples:

Mi familia **está en** Inglaterra	*My family is in England*
Los viajeros **están en** el avión	*The travellers are in the aeroplane*
La panadería **esta allí enfrente**	*The baker's is across the road*
La carnicería **está al lado de** la farmacia	*The butcher's is next to the chemist's*

Sometimes **estar** may be used with other persons of the verb:

Estoy en la cocina	*I'm in the kitchen*
Estamos en París	*We're in Paris*

See also page 201 of the **Grammar reference**.

2 Interrogative word *dónde*

Dónde (*where*), as an interrogative word, is used to enquire about location. It normally precedes the third person singular or plural of **estar**, but it may also be used with other persons of the verb. Here are some examples:

¿**Dónde** está Bilbao?	*Where's Bilbao?*
Está en el norte	*It's in the north*
¿**Dónde** están tus amigos?	*Where are your friends?*
Están en México	*They are in Mexico*
¿**Dónde** estás?	*Where are you?*
Estoy en el jardín	*I'm in the garden*

3 Words and phrases used in the expression of location and distance

To say where or how far a place is you will need prepositions, that is, words such as **en**, *in, on, at*, **entre**, *between* (see **Glossary of grammatical terms**). Some prepositions combine with adverbs of place, for example **enfrente**, *opposite*, to form prepositional phrases. The following list contains the most common prepositions and phrases used for expressing location and distance.

a (on, to)

Está **a** la izquierda/derecha	*It's on the left/right*
Está **a** la izquierda de la calle Mayor	*It's to the left of the calle Mayor*
Está **a** dos manzanas* de aquí	*It's two blocks from here*
Está **a** 20 km de aquí	*It's 20 km from here*

* The Spanish word for *block*; Latin Americans use **cuadra**.

en (in, on, at)

Está **en** la calle Alfonso X	*It's in Alfonxo X Street*
Está **en** la mesa	*It's on the table*
Él está **en** la escuela	*He's at school*

entre (between)

La universidad está **entre** la iglesia y el banco	*The university is between the church and the bank*

sobre (on, over, on top of, above)

Está **sobre** el escritorio	*It's on the desk*
Está **sobre** la ciudad	*It's over the city*
Está **sobre** él	*It's on top of him*
Está **sobre** tu cabeza	*It's above your head*

Notice that **en** and **sobre** are interchangeable in **está sobre/en el escritorio** (*it's on the desk*).

al final de (at the end of)

La tienda está **al final de** la calle	*The shop is at the end of the street*

al lado de (next to)

Mi casa está **al lado de** la estación	*My house is next to the station*

cerca de (near)

El cine está **cerca del** mercado	*The cinema is near the market*

debajo de (under, underneath)

Los zapatos están **debajo de** la cama	*The shoes are under the bed*

dentro de (within, inside)

El perro está **dentro de** la casa

The dog is inside the house

detrás de (behind)

La gasolinera está **detrás de** la estación

The service station is behind the station

enfrente de (opposite)

La zapatería está **enfrente de** la papelería

The shoe shop is opposite the stationer's

fuera de (outside)

El portero está **fuera del** edificio

The porter is outside the building

lejos de (far)

Sevilla está **lejos de** Bilbao

Seville is far from Bilbao

The words **aquí**, *here*, **allí**, *there*, and **ahí**, *there*, also express location:

El billete está aquí   *The ticket is here*
Correos está allí   *The post office is there*
Carlos está ahí   *Carlos is there*

Ahí indicates closer proximity than **allí**.

The words **acá**, *here*, and **allá**, *there*, are more frequent in Latin America:

¡Ven **acá**!   *Come here!*
Están **allá**   *They're there*

4 *Ser* to refer to the location of events

To ask and answer questions regarding the location of events, as in *Where's the party?* and *The party is in my flat*, we use **ser** rather than **estar**. Here are some examples:

¿Dónde es la fiesta?   *Where's the party?*
La fiesta es en mi piso   *The party is in my flat*
¿Dónde es la clase?   *Where's the class?*
La clase es aquí   *The class is here*

Remember

When *to be* means *to be held* or *to happen* it must be translated into Spanish as **ser**. (See also page 200 of the **Grammar reference**.)

5 Other verbs denoting location

Encontrarse, hallarse (to be, to be situated)

These two verbs are used in more formal contexts, especially in writing. Both are reflexive (see Unit 9); **encontrarse** is also a stem-changing verb (see Unit 8):

¿Dónde **se encuentra** Perú?	*Where's Peru?*
Se encuentra en Sudamérica	*It's in South America*
¿Dónde **se encuentran/hallan** las islas?	*Where are the islands?*
Se encuentran/hallan en el Atlántico	*They are in the Atlantic*

Estar situado (to be situated)

In this expression, **situado** must agree in gender (masculine or feminine) and number (singular or plural) with the noun it refers to:

La ciudad está situada al norte	*The city is/is situated in the north*
Los Andes están situados en Sudamérica	*The Andes are/are situated in South America*

In context

1 Looking for a bank.

Turista	Perdone, ¿hay algún banco por aquí?
Guardia	Sí, hay uno en la calle Mayor.
Turista	¿Dónde está la calle Mayor?
Guardia	Es la segunda calle a la izquierda. El banco está al lado del cine.
Turista	Muchas gracias.
Guardia	De nada.

la segunda calle	*the second street*
el guardia	*policeman*

2 On the way to the airport.

Conductor	Perdone, ¿cuál es la carretera para el aeropuerto?
Transeúnte	Es la próxima a la derecha.
Conductor	¿A qué distancia está el aeropuerto más o menos?
Transeúnte	Está a unos veinte kilómetros.
Conductor	Muchas gracias.
Transeúnte	No hay de qué.

el conductor	driver
el transeúnte	passer-by
no hay de qué	don't mention it
unos	about

Practice

1 You are trying to find your way around a Spanish town. What questions would you need to ask to get these replies? Look at the map and then ask the questions.

a Está en la calle Real, al lado de la plaza.
b Sí, hay dos, uno está en la calle Mayor, al lado de Correos, y el otro está en la calle Miramar, enfrente de la gasolinera.
c Está detrás del cine.
d Está en la próxima esquina, a la derecha, enfrente de la plaza.

2 How would you reply to these questions? Look at the map and answer.

a ¿Hay algún banco por aquí?
b ¿Dónde está la gasolinera?
c ¿Dónde está el museo?
d ¿Dónde está el hotel Sol?

06

expressing possession

In this unit you will learn how to
- express possession
- ask questions regarding possession

Language points
- possessive adjectives and pronouns
- using *de* to indicate possession
- expressing possession with *tener*
- definite article to express possession
- *pertenecer*

Key sentences

We can express possession in a variety of ways in English, for example: *That is my house, It's mine, Whose car is that?, It's Peter's, Have you got a computer?, I don't have one.* Spanish also has a number of ways of expressing possession. These involve some of the constructions learned in previous units.

Expressing possession

Ésta es **mi/su** bicicleta	*This is my/his/her bicycle*
Tus/sus llaves están aquí	*Your/his/her keys are here*
Nuestras/vuestras maletas son ésas	*Our/your suitcases are those*
El dinero es **mío/tuyo**	*The money is mine/yours*
La carpeta **de Ana** es la azul	*Ana's file is the blue one*
Tenemos/tienen una casa	*We/they have a house*

Asking questions regarding possession

¿**De quién** es este periódico?	*Whose newspaper is this one?*
¿**A quién** pertenece la propiedad?	*Who does the property belong to?*
¿**Tiene Vd./tienes** coche?	*Have you got a car?*

Grammar summary

1 Possessive adjectives and pronouns

To express possession we may, as in English, use possessives. Spanish has two sets of possessives: short forms such as **mi**, *my*, **tu**, *your* (familiar) and long forms such as **mío**, *mine*, **tuyo**, *yours* (familiar).

Short forms

Short forms function as adjectives and they agree in number (singular or plural) with the noun they accompany, but only those ending in -o in the masculine singular (**nuestro, vuestro**) agree in gender (masculine or feminine). Note that this agreement is with the *noun possessed*, not with the owner

mi	mis	*my*
tu	tus	*your* (familiar)
su	sus	*your* (formal), *his/her/its*
nuestro/a	nuestros/as	*our*
vuestro/a	vuestros/as	*your* (familiar)
su	sus	*your* (formal), *their*

Ésta es **mi** agenda	*This is my diary*
¿Has visto **mis** llaves?	*Have you seen my keys?*
Nuestro hijo llegó ayer	*Our son arrived yesterday*
Vuestra idea es estupenda	*Your idea is great*

Long forms

Long forms can function as pronouns, in place of a noun which is understood, or as adjectives. They agree in number (singular or plural) and gender (masculine or feminine) with the noun possessed.

mío/a	míos/as	*mine*
tuyo/a	tuyos/as	*yours* (familiar)
suyo/a	suyos/as	*yours* (formal), *his/hers/its*
nuestro/a	nuestros/as	*ours*
vuestro/a	vuestros/as	*yours* (familiar)
suyo/a	suyos/as	*yours* (formal), *theirs*

Note that in these examples the possessive pronoun is preceded by a definite article (**el, la, los, las**):

Me encanta su jardín, pero **el nuestro** es más grande	*I love his/her garden, but ours is larger*
¿Son éstas sus maletas?	*Are these your suitcases?*
No, **las nuestras** son ésas	*No, ours are those*

But no definite article is needed when the possessive pronoun is introduced by **ser**, *to be*, or when **ser** is understood, except after a preposition (words like **en**, *in*, **con**, *with*):

¿Es **tuyo** ese dinero?	*Is this money yours?*
Sí, (es) **mío**	*Yes, it's mine*
¿La fiesta será en **tu** casa?	*Will the party be in your house?*
Sí, será en **la mía**	*Yes, it will be in mine*

In the examples which follow long forms are acting as adjectives and are used without a definite article:

Es un amigo **mío**	He's a friend of mine
Ayer murió una tía **suya**	An aunt of his/hers died yesterday
Muy señor **mío**	Dear Sir
Muy señores **nuestros**	Dear Sirs

2 Using *de* to indicate possession

Another frequent way of expressing possession in Spanish is by using the construction **de** + name:

La casa **de** Mónica	Mónica's house
El libro **de** José	José's book

This construction with **de** is also used in order to avoid the ambiguity that may arise with third person possessive adjectives and pronouns, **su** and **suyo**.

Compare:

Su apartamento	Your (formal)/his/her/their apartment
El apartamento **de ella**	Her apartment
Un primo **suyo**	A cousin of yours (formal)/his/hers/theirs
Un primo **de él**	A cousin of his

3 ¿*De quién...*? (Whose...?)

To say *Whose is it?*, use the expression ¿**De quién es**? For *Whose are they?*, use ¿**De quién son**? To answer, use the construction **ser** + **de** + person/personal pronoun or **ser** + possessive:

¿**De quién** es este bolígrafo?	Whose is this ballpoint pen?
Es de Sofía /ella	It's Sofía's/hers
¿**De quién** son esos libros?	Whose books are those?
Son de Antonio	They are Antonio's
¿**De quién** es esto?	Whose is this?
Es mío/nuestro	Its mine/ours

4 Expressing possession with *tener*

Tener (*to have*) indicates possession in sentences such as the following:

Tienen mucho dinero	They have a lot of money
Tiene una casa en el campo	He/She has a house in the country
¿**Tienes** coche?	Do you have a car?
No, no **tengo**	No, I don't have one

5 Definite articles to express possession

The possessive is often substituted by a definite article when the object of the sentence is an item of clothing or a part of the body. For example:

Ella se lavó **las** manos	*She washed her hands*
Él se quitó **los** zapatos	*He took off his shoes*
Nos quitamos **las** chaquetas	*We took off our jackets*

6 *Pertenecer* (to belong)

Although it is less frequent, possession may also be expressed with **pertenecer** (*to belong*).

¿A quién **pertenece** esta casa?	*Who does this house belong to?*
Pertenece a un señor muy rico	*It belongs to a very rich gentleman*
¿A quién **pertenecen** esos edificios?	*Who do those buildings belong to?*
Pertenecen a una firma inglesa	*They belong to an English firm*

Pertenecer is conjugated like **conocer**, *to know* (see page 56).

In context

1 A hotel porter is helping a tourist with her luggage.

Portero	¿Cuál es su equipaje?
Turista	El mío es aquél.
Portero	¿Este maletín también es suyo?
Turista	No, no es mío, es de mi amiga. El mío es el negro.
Portero	¿Dónde está su coche?
Turista	Está en el aparcamiento.

2 Talking about the family.

Marisol	¿Cómo están tus hijos?
Isabel	Muy bien, ¿y los tuyos?
Marisol	Pablo está un poco resfriado, pero Teresa está bien. Ahora está en casa de sus abuelos. Pablo está solo en casa.
Isabel	Los míos están en la piscina con sus amigos.

está un poco resfriado	*he has a slight cold*

3 Alfonso sees a typed note on his desk. It has been left there by his colleague Roberto.

Alfonso,

Hoy es el cumpleaños de mi mujer y tenemos una pequeña fiesta en nuestro nuevo apartamento. Tú eres nuestro invitado de honor. No faltes. Nuestra dirección es Ismael Valdés Vergara 640 B.

Roberto

hoy	*today*
el invitado de honor	*guest of honour*

In dialogues 1 and 2, note the use of possessive pronouns preceded by the definite article (**el, los**). In each of these phrases the noun is understood, therefore it has been omitted: **el** (**equipaje**) **mío** (*mine, my luggage*), **el** (**maletín**) **mío** (*mine, my suitcase*), **los** (**hijos**) **tuyos** (*yours, your children*).

Practice

1 Fill in the gaps with a possessive or other suitable words expressing possession.

a Perdone Vd., ¿es suya está carta? Sí, es...
b ¿...... quién son esos libros? Son ... Carlos.
c Buenas tardes, señor Díaz, ¿cómo está ... familia?
d Hola María, te presento a ... marido. Y éstos son ... hijos, Pablo y Carmen.
e Éstas no son mis maletas . Las ... son ésas.
f ¿Es ésa la casa de Cristina y José? No, la ... es la que está en la esquina.
g ¿A quién ... esa empresa?
h Tienes que lavarte ... manos porque vamos a comer.

2 Mario received the following letter from a friend. Can you fill in the gaps in it with a suitable possessive?

Querido Mario:

Muchas gracias por (1) ... carta y muchas gracias también por (2) ... invitación para este verano. Desgraciadamente me es imposible ir, porque en agosto llega Mónica, una gran amiga (3) ..., de Nueva York.

¿Cómo están (4) … padres? Los (5) … están muy bien.
Ahora están de vacaciones en (6) … apartamento de la
playa. Y (7) … novia, ¿cómo está? ¿Cómo se llama? No
recuerdo (8) … nombre.

Mario, ahora tenemos teléfono en casa. (9) … número es el
675 4321. Pero yo no tengo el (10) … ¿Cuál es tu número?

3 Write sentences about Juan, Ana/Luis and you, using **tener**.

a Juan **tiene tarjetas de crédito.** (tarjetas de crédito)
b Ana y Luis…………………… (tarjetas de crédito)
c Yo ………………………… (tarjetas de crédito)
d Juan ……………………… (una casa)
e Ana y Luis…………………… (una casa)
f Yo ………………………… (una casa)
g Juan ……………………… (coche/carro, L. Am.)
h Ana y Luis…………………… (coche/carro)
i Yo ………………………… (coche/carro)

	Juan	**Ana/Luis**	**tú**
	✓	✗	?
	✗	✓	?
	✓	✓	?

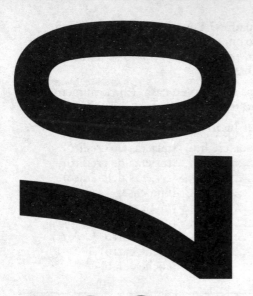

07 expressing obligation and needs

In this unit you will learn how to
- express obligation and needs
- ask questions with regard to obligation and needs

Language points
- *tener que*
- *necesitar*
- *deber*
- *hay que*
- *hacer falta*
- *ser necesario*
- present tense of 1st and 2nd conjugation verbs

Key sentences

We can express obligation and need in English in a variety of ways, for example: *I have to go, We must tell them, She needs to work more, One has to accept it, What do you have to do?* Spanish also has a number of ways of expressing obligation and need, as you will see from the following examples and grammar notes.

Expressing obligation and need

Tengo/tienen que salir	*I/they have to go out*
Debo/debemos estar allí a las 6.00	*I/we must be there at 6.00*
Necesita/necesito hablar con Vd.	*He/she needs/I need to talk to you*

Expressing obligation and need in impersonal terms

Hay que hacer un esfuerzo	*One needs to make an effort*
No hace falta decírselo	*We/You don't need to tell him/her*
Es necesario esperar	*It's necessary to wait*
Se necesita tener paciencia	*One needs to have patience*

Asking questions with regard to obligation and need

¿Qué tienes/tenéis que hacer?	*What do you have to do?*
¿Qué debo/debemos decir?	*What must I/we say?*
¿Qué necesitas/necesitan?	*What do you/they need?*
¿Hace falta/hay que comprar algo?	*Do we need to buy anything?*

Grammar summary

1 *Tener que* (to have to)

Tener que is the verb most frequently used in the expression of obligation and need. As in English, it is used with an infinitive:

¿Qué **tienes que** hacer?	*What do you have to do?*
Tengo que trabajar	*I have to work*

| ¿Qué **tenéis que** comprar? | *What do you have to buy?* |
| **Tenemos que** comprar pan | *We have to buy bread* |

For the full forms of **tener** in the present tense see Unit 4.

2 *Necesitar* (to need) and present tense of 1st conjugation verbs

To say what we need or what we need to do, we may use **necesitar** (*to need*), followed by a noun, e.g. **necesito dinero** (*I need money*), a pronoun, e.g. **necesito ésos** (*I need those*) or an infinitive, e.g. **necesito hablar con él** (*I need to speak to him*). **Necesitar** is a regular verb whose infinitive ends in **-ar**. Verbs which finish in **-ar** are known as 1st conjugation verbs.

Here are the present tense forms of **necesitar**. Bear in mind that the endings will be the same for all regular **-ar** verbs.

Singular		**Plural**	
necesito	*I need*	necesitamos	*we need*
necesitas	*you need* (fam.)	necesitáis	*you need* (fam.)
necesita	*you need* (pol.)	necesitan	*you need* (pol.)
	he/she/it needs		*they need*

¿Cuánto tiempo **necesitas**?	*How much time do you need?*
Necesito un mes	*I need a month*
¿**Necesitan** Vds. hablar con alguien?	*Do you need to talk to somebody?*
Necesitamos hablar con Vd.	*We need to talk to you*

3 *Deber* (must, to have to) and present tense of 2nd conjugation verbs

Deber is followed directly by an infinitive. It is a regular verb whose infinitive ends in **-er**. Verbs which finish in **-er** are known as 2nd conjugation verbs.

Here are the present tense forms of **deber**. Bear in mind that the endings will be the same for all regular **-er** verbs.

Singular		Plural	
debo	*I must, have to*	debemos	*we must, have to*
debes	*you must, have to* (fam.)	debéis	*you must, have to* (fam.)
debe	*you must, have to* (pol.)	deben	*you must, have to* (pol.)
	he/she/it must, has to		*they must, have to*

¿Qué **debo** hacer?	*What must I do?*
Debes decir la verdad	*You must tell the truth*
Debemos volver	*We must come back*
Deben esperar	*They must wait*

4 Expressing obligation and need in impersonal terms

To express obligation and need in an impersonal way, use the following constructions:

Hay que + infinitive

Hay que tener mucho cuidado	*One has to be very careful*
No **hay que** hacer nada	*You don't have to do anything*

Hacer falta + infinitive/noun

Hace falta estudiar mucho	*One needs to study a lot*
Hace falta mucho dinero	*One needs a lot of money*

Se + *necesita* + infinitive/noun

Se necesita ser muy capaz	*You need to be very capable*
Se necesita dependienta	*We need a shop assistant*

Ser necesario

You can use this expression on its own or with an infinitive. By and large, however, this construction is much less frequent than the equivalent English expression *to be necessary*.

Es necesario abrir la ventana	*It's necessary to open the window*
¿Es necesario hacerlo?	*Is it necessary to do it?*
No, no es necesario	*No, it's not necessary*

5 Expressing strong need

To express strong need you can use the following expressions
with ser, *to be*: ser preciso, *to be necessary*, ser imprescindible,
ser esencial, ser indispensable, ser fundamental, *to be
essential/vital*:

Es preciso recordarle	*It's necessary to remind him/her*
Es imprescindible viajar	*It's essential to travel*
Es esencial tenerlo aquí	*It's essential to have him/it here*
Es indispensable ir solo	*It's essential to go alone*
Es fundamental no decir nada	*It's vital not to say anything*

In context

1 Enquiring about a visa for a Spanish-speaking country.

Secretaria	Buenos días. ¿Qué desea?
Viajero	¿Qué tengo que hacer para conseguir un visado para Venezuela?
Secretaria	¿Qué pasaporte tiene Vd.?
Viajero	Español.
Secretaria	Tiene que rellenar esta solicitud y traer su pasaporte con tres fotografías.
Viajero	¿Necesito traer una carta de mi empresa?
Secretaria	¿Es un viaje de negocios?
Viajero	Sí, es un viaje de negocios.
Secretaria	Sí, en ese caso debe traer una carta de su empresa.

conseguir	*to get*
rellenar una solicitud	*to fill in a form*
la empresa	*firm*
un viaje de negocios	*a business trip*
en ese caso	*in that case*

2 Elena, a secretary, describes her duties in a letter to a friend.

*... hay que estar en la oficina a las 9.00. Primero
tengo que leer la correspondencia de mi jefe y
responder a las cartas más urgentes. A veces
debo asistir a reuniones y tomar notas y de vez
en cuando tengo que salir para ir al banco o para
visitar a algún cliente ...*

a veces	sometimes
asistir	to attend
tomar notas	to take notes
de vez en cuando	from time to time

Notice the use of **para** in these phrases:

para conseguir un visado	to (in order to) get a visa
para ir al banco	(in order) to go to the bank
para visitar a algún cliente	(in order) to visit some client

For an explanation of the use of the preposition **a** in **visitar a algún cliente** *to visit a client*, see page 86.

Practice

1 Here are some sentences expressing obligation and need. Can you fill in the gaps in each word with the missing letters?

a T – n – – o – que salir muy pronto.
b – – y que estar allí al mediodía.
c No d – – – s decir nada.
d ¿Qué n – – e – – t – Vd.?
e – a – e   f – l – – hablar español.
f Es n – c – s – – – o trabajar mucho.
g Se   – e – e – – t – secretaria que hable español.
h Es   i – – r – s – i – d – – l – estudiar más.

2 Eloísa's problems need sorting out. What does she have to do to solve them? Match each problem with a suitable solution.

a Estoy muy delgada.
b Mi madre no está bien.
c No tengo suficiente dinero.
d No estoy muy contenta en mi trabajo.
e Mi inglés no es muy bueno.
f La casa está sucia.

1 Tienes que hacer un esfuerzo y estudiar más.
2 Es necesario limpiarla.
3 Debes buscar otro.
4 Hay que llamar al médico.
5 Tienes que comer más.
6 Tienes que trabajar.

08

talking about the present

In this unit you will learn how to
- describe states which are true in the present
- refer to events which are present but not in progress
- refer to events taking place the present
- express timeless ideas
- ask questions regarding present states and events

Language points
- 3rd conjugation verbs
- irregular verbs
- stem-changing verbs
- present continuous (*estar* + gerund)
- *llevar* + gerund
- *hacer* in time phrases

Key sentences

In this unit dealing with the present you will have a chance to review some of the constructions learned in previous units, such as the present tense of -**ar** and -**er** verbs, which you learned in Unit 7. The sentences and grammar summary which follow will take you a step further by showing you how to use the present tense of verbs ending in -**ir** as well as other verbs which do not follow a fixed pattern. You will also learn other constructions used in Spanish for talking about the present.

Describing states which are true in the present

Hoy hace calor/frío	*It's warm/cold today*
Elena está enferma/cansada	*Elena is ill/tired*

Referring to events which are present but not in progress

Escucha ese ruido	*Listen to that noise*
Alguien llama/viene	*Someone's calling/coming*

Referring to events taking place in the present

El niño duerme/está durmiendo	*The child is sleeping*
Estudio/estoy estudiando	*I'm studying*

Expressing timeless ideas

Es difícil/caro	*It's difficult/expensive*
No me gusta/importa	*I don't like it/mind*

Asking questions regarding present states and events

¿Cómo estás/están?	*How are you/they?*
¿Oyes ese ruido?	*Do you hear that noise?*
¿Qué pasa/está pasando?	*What's wrong/is happening?*

Grammar summary

1 3rd conjugation verbs

Verbs whose infinitive ends in -ir, for example vivir (*to live*) and escribir (*to write*), are known as 3rd conjugation verbs. Here are the present tense forms of vivir:

vivir (*to live*)			
Singular		**Plural**	
vivo	*I live*	vivimos	*we live*
vives	*you live* (fam.)	vivís	*you live* (fam.)
vive	*you live* (pol.)	viven	*you live* (pol.)
	he/she/it lives		*they live*

¿Dónde vives?	*Where do you live?*
Vivo en Londres	*I live in London*
¿Subes?	*Are you going up?*
Subo ahora mismo	*I'm going up right away*
El banco abre a las 3.00	*The bank opens at 3.00*
¿Qué escribes?	*What are you writing?*
Escribo una carta	*I'm writing a letter*

(For 1st and 2nd conjugation verbs see Unit 7.)

2 Irregular verbs

There are many verbs in Spanish which do not follow a fixed pattern in their conjugation. They are irregular. In the present tense, some verbs are irregular only in the 1st person singular. Here is a list of the most common. Those marked with an asterisk (*) are also stem-changing verbs (see pages 57–9).

-ar verbs	
dar *to give*	doy *I give*
-er verbs	
conocer *to know*	conozco *I know*
hacer *to do, make*	hago *I do, make*
parecer *to seem*	parezco *I seem*
pertenecer *to belong*	pertenezco *I belong*
poner *to put*	pongo *I put*
saber *to know*	sé *I know*
tener* *to have*	tengo *I have*

| traer *to bring* | traigo *I bring* |
| ver *to see* | veo *I see* |

-ir verbs

conducir *to drive*	conduzco *I drive*
decir* *to say, tell*	digo *I say, tell*
oír *to hear*	oigo *I hear*
salir *to go out*	salgo *I go out*
venir* *to come*	vengo *I come*

Oír has other changes: **i** changes to **y** in the 2nd and 3rd person singular and the 3rd person plural:

oigo	oímos
oyes	oís
oye	oyen

Some verbs, for example **ser** (*to be*), **estar** (*to be*), **haber** (*to have*, auxiliary verb) and **ir** (*to go*) are highly irregular. (For the present tense of **ser** sec Unit 1, for **estar** Unit 3, for **haber** Unit 19.) Here are the present tense forms of **ir**:

ir (*to go*)			
voy	*I go*	vamos	*we go*
vas	*you go* (fam.)	vais	*you go* (fam.)
va	*you go* (pol.)	van	*you go* (pol.)
	he/she/it goes		*they go*

¿Adónde vas?	*Where are you going?*
Voy al cine	*I'm going to the cinema*
Allí va Manuel	*There goes Manuel*

For a list of the most common irregular verbs in all tenses see pages 203–6.

3 Stem-changing verbs

Some verbs undergo a change in the stem (the main part of the verb without its ending) which occurs only when the stem is stressed. Therefore, the 1st and 2nd person plural are not affected by this change. Stem-changing verbs have the same endings as regular verbs.

Here is a list of the most common stem-changing verbs in the present tense:

Verbs which change *e* to *ie*			
-ar		**-er**	
cerrar	to *close, shut*	encender	to *light, turn on*
despertar(se)	to *wake up*	entender	to *understand*
empezar	to *begin*	perder	to *lose*
nevar	to *snow*	querer	to *want*
pensar	to *think*	tener	to *have*
	-ir		
herirse	to *hurt oneself*	sentir(se)	to *feel*
preferir	to *prefer*	venir	to *come*

Here is an example of one of the above verbs in all its forms:

pensar (*to think*)			
pienso	*I think*	pensamos	*we think*
piensas	*you think* (fam.)	pensáis	*you think* (fam.)
piensa	*you think* (pol.)	piensan	*you think* (pol.)
	he/she thinks		*they think*

Verbs which change *o* to *ue*			
-ar		**-er**	
acostarse	to *go to bed*	devolver	to *return, give back*
acordarse	to *remember*	doler	to *hurt, feel pain*
comprobar	to *check*	llover	to *rain*
contar	to *tell, count*	moverse	to *move*
encontrar	to *find*	poder	to *be able*
mostrar	to *show*	soler	to *be accustomed to*
recordar	to *remember*	volver	to *return*
rogar	to *ask, beg*		
	-ir		
dormir(se)	to *sleep, go to sleep*	morir(se)	to *die*

Jugar, whose stem has a **u**, also changes into **ue**:

juego	*I play*
juegas	*you play* (fam.)
juega	*you play* (pol.) *he/she/it plays*
juegan	*you/they play*

Here is one of the above verbs in its present tense forms:

volver (to return)			
vuelvo	*I return*	volvemos	*we return*
vuelves	*you return* (fam.)	volvéis	*you return* (fam.)
vuelve	*you return* (pol.)	vuelven	*you return* (pol.)
	he/she returns		*they return*

Verbs which change e to i			
conseguir	*to get*	reír(se)	*to laugh*
corregir	*to correct*	repetir	*to repeat*
elegir	*to choose*	seguir	*to follow, continue*
pedir	*to ask (for)*	servir	*to serve*

Notice also the change in the 1st person singular of the following verbs:

conseguir → consigo   elegir → elijo

corregir → corrijo   seguir → sigo

Here is **pedir** in its present tense forms:

pedir (to ask (for))			
pido	*I ask*	pedimos	*we ask*
pides	*you ask* (fam.)	pedís	*you ask* (fam.)
pide	*you ask* (pol.)	piden	*you ask* (pol.)
	he/she asks		*they ask*

4 Present continuous (*estar* + gerund)

To say what you are doing at the moment of speaking you use **estar** followed by a gerund. This is formed by adding **-ando** to the stem of **-ar** verbs and **-iendo** to that of **-er** and **-ir** verbs: **hablar** → **hablando, hacer** → **haciendo, escribir** → **escribiendo**:

Está hablando con el jefe   *He/she is speaking to the boss*
¿Qué estás haciendo?   *What are you doing?*
Estoy escribiendo una carta   *I'm writing a letter*

Spelling changes in the gerund

Verbs ending in **-ir** which change the stem from **e** to **i** (see para. 3 above) also show this change in the gerund, e.g. **pedir** → **pidiendo**.

Verbs ending in **-ir** which change **e** into **ie** (see para. 3 above) also take **i** in the gerund, e.g. **venir** → **viniendo**.

Verbs ending in **-ir** and certain **-er** verbs which change **o** to **ue** (see para. 3 above) take **u** in the gerund, e.g. **dormir** → **durmiendo, poder** → **pudiendo**.

Using the present continuous

• In contrast with the present tense, to make it perfectly clear that we are referring to an action which is taking place at the time, for example **¿Qué estás haciendo?**, *What are you doing?* instead of **¿Qué haces?**, *What do you do?* or *What are you doing?*

• To emphasize some kind of change in the action in relation with the past, as in **Estoy viviendo en California**, *I'm living in California*.

• To refer to an action which has been taking place over a period of time including the present, for example **Está lloviendo desde anoche**, *It's been raining since last night*.

• To express disapproval or surprise, for example **¡Pero qué estás diciendo!**, *But what are you saying!*

5 Other ways of referring to the present

To refer to events which began at some point in the past but which are still in progress we can use the following constructions:

Llevar + gerund

¿Cuánto tiempo llevas trabajando aquí?	*How long have you been working here?*
Llevo un año (trabajando) aquí	*I've been working here for a year*
Llevamos dos horas esperando	*We've been waiting for two hours*

Hace + time phrase + que + present tense

¿Cuánto tiempo hace que vives en Madrid?	*How long have you been living in Madrid?*
Hace seis meses que vivo allí	*I've been living there for six months*
Hace dos años que estudio español	*I've been studying Spanish for two years*

Note the following alternative to the last two sentences:

Vivo allí desde hace seis meses	*I've been living there for six months*
Estudio español desde hace dos años	*I've been studying Spanish for two years*

In context

1 Here is an extract from a postcard describing a holiday.

Querida Carolina:

Te escribo desde Río. Estoy aquí de vacaciones con mi familia. Hace muchísimo calor y estamos todos muy morenos. Río es fantástico. Los chicos están muy contentos. Ahora están jugando con unos amigos mientras yo escribo y escucho música brasileña.
¡Qué tranquila estoy! No te imaginas ...

estamos morenos	*we are tanned*
brasileño/a	*Brazilian*
¡qué tranquila estoy!	*how relaxed I am*
no te imaginas	*you can't imagine*

2 An appointment with the manager.

Cliente   Buenos días. Tengo una cita con el gerente. Me llamo Hugo Pérez.

Secretaria   Un momento, por favor, señor Pérez. El gerente está hablando con unos clientes.

Cliente   ¿Y la señora Martínez está?

Secretaria   La señora Martínez ya no trabaja aquí. Está trabajando en una firma en Barcelona. Ah, allí viene el gerente ...

tengo una cita	*I have an appointment*
ya no	*not any longer*

Practice

1 Fill in the gaps with the appropriate present tense form of the infinitive in brackets.

a Carlos (jugar) muy bien al tenis. Yo no (saber) jugar.
b En Galicia (llover) mucho, pero no (nevar).

c Gloria no (entender) bien el español.

d (Yo, conocer) mucha gente en España porque (ir) allí en mis vacaciones.

e (Yo) no (encontrar) mis llaves. No (recordar) dónde están.

f Luis (empezar) a trabajar a las 9.00. Nosotros (empezar) a las 9.30.

2 How would you ask Ignacio how long he has been doing each of the following and how would he reply? Use the construction with **hace** and the phrases given below.

a Vivir en Madrid – 10 años.
b Trabajar en la misma empresa – 8 años.
c Estudiar inglés – 5 años.
d Conocer a Isabel – 3 años y medio.
e Jugar al tenis – 2 años.
f Hacer yoga – 6 meses.

Now try saying how long you have been doing certain things, for example studying Spanish or working.

3 Can you say what these people are doing? Match each phrase with the corresponding picture and fill in the correct form of **estar** + gerund. (*Ejemplo*: 1–c Está escuchando.)

1 (escuchar) música
2 (comer) en el campo
3 (cocinar)
4 (leer) el periódico
5 (nadar) en la piscina
6 (jugar) al fútbol

a

d

b

e

c

f

09
talking about habitual actions

In this unit you will learn how to
- ask for and give information about habitual actions
- say how often you or others do certain things
- ask how often people do certain things
- ask and state what time something is done

Language points
- reflexive verbs
- adverbs ending in *-mente*
- frequency adverbs
- preposition *a* in time phrases
- *soler* + infinitive
- *acostumbrar* + infinitive

Key sentences

In this unit you will learn to talk about things you do normally, such as your daily routine. This will involve the revision of the present tense as well as the introduction of new forms of the verb. By the end of this unit you should also be familiar with the Spanish equivalent of words which express frequency, such as *always, never, often*.

Look at these examples and then read the grammar notes which follow.

Asking and giving information about habitual actions

¿Qué haces los domingos/
fines de semana?

*What do you do on Sundays/
at weekends?*

Leo/escucho música/salgo

I read/listen to music/go out

Saying how often you or others do certain things

Siempre/nunca llega a la
hora

*He/she always/never arrives on
time*

A veces/de vez en cuando
nos invitan

*They invite us sometimes/from
time to time*

Asking people how often they do certain things

¿Viene Vd. aquí a menudo/
siempre?

*Do you often/always come
here?*

¿Cuántas veces por semana/
mes la ves?

*How many times a week/
month do you see her?*

Asking and stating what time something is done

¿A qué hora cenas/te
acuestas?

*What time do you have
dinner/go to bed?*

¿A qué hora empieza/
termina?

*What time does he/she/it
start/finish?*

Grammar summary

1 Reflexive verbs

A reflexive verb is one that is normally indicated by -se added to the infinitive, e.g. levantarse (*to get up*), lavarse (*to wash*). Se is sometimes translated into English as oneself, e.g., alegrarse (*to enjoy oneself*), but often it is not expressed at all. The reflexive pronouns me, te, se, nos, os, se could be said to correspond to forms such as *myself, yourself, himself, herself*, etc.

Reflexive verbs are conjugated in the usual way but with a reflexive pronoun preceding the verb. For example:

	levantarse (*to get up*)		
me levanto	*I get up*	nos levantamos	*we get up*
te levantas	*you get up* (fam.)	os levantáis	*you get up* (fam.)
se levanta	*you get up* (pol.)	se levantan	*you get up* (pol.)
	he/she gets up		*they get up*

Los sábados siempre me levanto tarde	*On Saturdays I always get up late*
Se levanta y se va al trabajo	*He/she gets up and goes to work*
Nos levantamos antes de las 6.00	*We get up before 6.00*

Position of reflexive pronouns

As explained earlier, reflexive pronouns normally precede the verb, but they are attached to the end of infinitives, gerunds (see Unit 8) and positive imperative forms (see Unit 20).

Antes de acostarse lee un rato.	*Before going to bed he/she reads for a while.*
Afeitándose, se cortó	*He cut himself while shaving.*
Levántate, es tarde.	*Get up, it's late.*

In a construction with a main verb followed by an infinitive or a gerund, the reflexive pronoun may either precede the main verb or be attached to the infinitive or gerund, as above.

Me voy a duchar, *or* Voy a ducharme.	*I'm going to take a shower.*
Nos tenemos que ir, *or* Tenemos que irnos.	*We have to leave.*

Some common reflexive verbs

There is a large number of reflexive verbs in Spanish. Here is a list of some of the most frequent. The (ie), (ue) or (i) next to the verb shows that its stem changes in the present tense (see Unit 8).

acostarse (ue)	*to go to bed*	levantarse	*to get up*
acordarse (ue)	*to remember*	marcharse	*to leave*
afeitarse	*to shave*	morirse (ue)	*to die*
alegrarse	*to be glad*	moverse (ue)	*to move*
bañarse	*to have a bath*	olvidarse	*to forget*
casarse	*to get married*	pararse	*to stop*
cortarse	*to cut oneself*	peinarse	*to comb one's*
despertarse (ie)	*to wake up*		*hair*
equivocarse	*to make a*	probarse (ue)	*to try on*
	mistake	reírse (i)	*to laugh*
hallarse	*to be (situated)*	sentarse (ie)	*to sit down*
irse	*to leave*	sentirse (ie)	*to feel*
lavarse	*to wash*		

2 Adverbs ending in -mente

In English we often form adverbs by adding *-ly* to an adjective, as in *normally* or *frequently*. In Spanish many adverbs are formed by adding -**mente** to the feminine form of the adjective, for example **rápida** (*rapid*) becomes **rápidamente** (*rapidly*); **lenta** (*slow*) becomes **lentamente** (*slowly*). Notice that if the adjective carries an accent, the accent is kept in the adverb.

If the adjective ends in a consonant, simply add -**mente**, for example, **fácil** (*easy*) becomes **fácilmente** (*easily*).

When there are two or more consecutive adverbs in -**mente** joined by a conjunction, e.g. **y** (*and*), **pero** (*but*), only the final one takes the ending -**mente**, for example:

Él trabaja rápida y
   eficiente**mente**

*He works rapidly and
   efficiently*

3 Frequency adverbs

The following adverbs and adverbial phrases are commonly used to say how often one does something:

frecuentemente	*frequently*
generalmente	*generally, usually*
normalmente	*normally*
usualmente	*usually*
a menudo	*often*
a veces	*sometimes*
de vez en cuando	*from time to time*
una vez, dos veces (por semana)	*once, twice (a week)*
siempre	*always*
nunca, jamás	*never*
todos los días (meses, años)	*every day (month, year)*
cada día (semana, mes, año)	*every day (week, month, year)*

Ella **nunca** sale de noche	*She never goes out at night*
Van a Sevilla **dos veces** al año	*They go to Seville twice a year*
La veo **a menudo**	*I see her often*
Nunca me llama	*He/she never calls me*
No me llama **nunca**	*He/she never calls me*

Notice the double negative when **nunca** is placed after a verb.

4 Preposition *a* in time phrases

Note the use of the preposition **a** in the expressions ¿a qué hora?, **a las** (time):

¿**A** qué hora sales de la oficina?	*What time do you leave the office?*
Salgo **a** las 7.00	*I leave at 7.00*

5 *Soler* + infinitive

We can also ask and answer questions about habitual actions by using the construction **soler** (o → ue) plus infinitive. **Soler** by itself translates into English as *to be in the habit of, usually...*

¿Qué **suele** hacer Vd. en el el verano?	*What do you usually do in the summer?*
Suelo salir de vacaciones	*I usually go on holiday*
¿Dónde **sueles** comer?	*Where do you normally eat?*
Suelo comer en un restaurante	*I usually eat in a restaurant*
Solemos trabajar hasta muy tarde	*We usually work until very late*

6 *Acostumbrar* + infinitive

Like **soler** + infinitive, **acostumbrar** + infinitive translates into English as *to be in the habit of* or *to be accustomed to*, *to usually* (*do*, etc.). Some speakers use this expression with the preposition **a** following the verb: **acostumbrar a** + infinitive. Both forms are correct:

Acostumbro (a) levantarme tarde	*I usually get up late*
No **acostumbramos** (a) hacer eso	*We don't usually do that*

In context

1 Read this extract from a letter in which Ignacio, a student, relates his daily activities to a new friend.

Estudio en un instituto de Granada y tengo clases de lunes a viernes por la mañana y por la tarde. Generalmente me levanto a eso de las 8.00 y me voy al instituto que está muy cerca de casa. Al mediodía vuelvo a casa a comer y a las 3.00 regreso al instituto. A las 6.00 termino las clases y vuelvo nuevamente a casa. A veces salgo con mis amigos...

a eso de	*around*
al mediodía	*at midday*

2 Alicia talks to a friend about her daily routine at work.

Cristóbal	¿Qué horario de trabajo tienes?
Alicia	Pues, no tengo un horario fijo, pero normalmente llego a la oficina a las 8.00 y estoy allí hasta las 4.00.
Cristóbal	¿Trabajas también los sábados?
Alicia	No, los sábados no trabajo. Generalmente voy con José, mi marido, al supermercado y por la tarde nos quedamos en casa. De vez en cuando cenamos fuera o vamos al cine.
Cristóbal	¿Y los domingos qué hacéis?
Alicia	Bueno, los domingos muchas veces vamos a la sierra. Allí tenemos una casa para pasar los fines de semana ...

un horario fijo	*fixed working hours*
fuera	*out*
muchas veces	*many times*
la sierra	*mountains*

Note the phrase **a eso de las** 8.00 (about 8.00).

Other ways of expressing approximate times are:

alrededor de las 8.00
sobre las 8.00
a las 8.00 aproximadamente.

These all mean *about 8.00*.

Practice

1 In a letter to a friend Marta describes her daily routine during her holidays. Fill in the gaps with a suitable verb from the list, using the appropriate form of the present tense.

ver – escribir – levantarse – ser – salir – llamar – desayunar – leer – volver – hacer – jugar – acostarse – ayudar – oír

En tu última carta me preguntas qué (1)... durante mis vacaciones. Bueno, mira, normalmente (2)... a las 8.30, después (3)..., generalmente un café y unas tostadas, y luego (4)... a mi madre en casa. A veces (5)... al supermercado a hacer la compra. Por la tarde (6)... la radio o (7)... la televisión y de vez en cuando (8)... al tenis con algún amigo. También (9)... mucho, especialmente revistas. Por la noche (10)... con mis amigos de paseo, y a eso de las 9.00 (11)... a casa a cenar. Después (12)... cartas o (13)... por teléfono a alguna amiga. Nunca (14)... antes de la medianoche.

Now try writing about your own daily routine.

2 What questions would you ask to get these replies? Use the familiar form.

a Normalmente me levanto a eso de las 7.00.
b Salgo de la oficina a las 6.00.
c Tengo clase de 7.00 a 8.00.
d No, no me acuesto tarde.
e Los fines de semana no hago nada especial.
f En mis vacaciones suelo ir a San Sebastián.

3 Here are some of the things Elena normally does during the week. Complete each sentence with an appropriate phrase from the list below, using the present tense.

| (hablar) por teléfono | (volver) a casa | (irse) al trabajo |
| (soler) ver la televisión | (preparar) la cena | (levantarse) |

a .... a las 7.10

b .... a las 7.45

c Por la mañana, en la oficina, ...

d A las 5.00 de la tarde ....

e Después de las 7.00 ....

f Por la noche ....

10

stating possibility, capacity and permission

In this unit you will learn how to
- state possibility or probability
- state capacity
- ask questions regarding possibility and capacity
- request, give and deny permission

Language points
- *poder* (+ infinitive)
- *saber* (+infinitive)
- *se* in impersonal sentences
- *ser posible* + infinitive

Key sentences

This unit focuses on the expression of possibility, capacity and permission, through the use of verbs such as **poder** and **saber**.

Stating possibility

Puede llover/ser difícil	*It may rain/be difficult*
Puede estar en casa/ocupado	*He may be at home/busy*

Stating capacity

No puedo hacerlo/explicarlo	*I can't do it/explain it*
No sé nadar/jugar al tenis	*I can't swim/play tennis*

Asking questions regarding possibility and capacity

¿Puedes venir/volver mañana?	*Can you come/return tomorrow?*
¿Sabes tocar el piano/jugar al ajedrez?	*Can you play the piano/chess?*

Requesting, giving and denying permission

¿Puedo fumar/aparcar aquí?	*May I smoke/park here?*
Aquí no se puede fumar/ aparcar	*You can't smoke/park here*

Grammar summary

1 *Poder* (+ infinitive) (can, be able to, may)

Poder, a verb whose stem changes from **o** to **ue** in the present tense (**puedo, puedes, puede, podemos, podéis, pueden**), is normally used with an infinitive to express possibility, capacity or permission. Here are some further examples:

Puede suceder	*It may happen* (possibility)
No **puedo** ayudarte	*I can't help you* (capacity)
¿**Puedo** pasar?	*May I come in?* (permission)

2 *Saber* (+ infinitive) (to be able to)

Saber (literally *to know*) is often used to express capacity or ability. Here are some further examples:

No sé cocinar	*I don't know how to cook*
Ella no **sabe** bailar	*She doesn't know how to dance*
¿**Sabes** tocar el piano?	*Do you know how to play the piano?*

3 *Se* in impersonal sentences

Impersonal sentences such as *Is it possible to go in?*, *Can one eat here?* and *One can't listen to music here* are expressed in Spanish through the word **se** followed by **poder** in the 3rd person singular plus an infinitive. Look at these examples:

¿**Se puede** entrar?	*Is it possible to go in?/ can one go in?*
¿**Se puede** comer aquí?	*Can one eat here?*
Aquí no **se puede** escuchar música	*One can't listen to music here*

There is more on the use of **se** in Unit 11.

4 *Ser* posible + infinitive

Possibility may also be expressed in Spanish with the phrase **es posible** plus infinitive, a construction which is much less frequent in Spanish than its English equivalent *it's possible*:

¿**Es posible** hablar con el señor Díaz?	*Is it possible to speak to señor Díaz?*
Lo siento, no **es posible**	*I'm sorry, it isn't possible*
¿**Es posible** reservar una habitación por teléfono?	*Is it possible to book a room on the phone?*
Por supuesto que **es posible**	*Of course it's possible*

In context

1 Where can we park?

Conductor Perdone, ¿se puede aparcar aquí?
Policía No señor, aquí no se puede.

Conductor	¿Dónde se puede aparcar?
Policía	En la plaza Mayor, al final de la calle.
Conductor	¿Puedo girar aquí?
Policía	Aquí no, pero puede girar en la próxima calle a la derecha y luego bajar hasta la plaza.
Conductor	Gracias.
Policía	De nada.

girar	*to turn*
bajar	*to go down*
hasta	*as far as, to*

2 What can one do in Barcelona?

Turista A	¿Qué se puede hacer en Barcelona?
Turista B	Se puede ir a algún museo, al museo de Picasso por ejemplo. También se puede visitar el Barrio Gótico, que es muy bonito. Puede ir al puerto, que está muy cerca de aquí …
Turista A	¿Y por la noche qué se puede hacer?
Turista B	Por la noche puede Vd. ir a algún espectáculo, al teatro o a la ópera por ejemplo, o tomar una copa en un bar …
Turista A	Y los fines de semana, ¿dónde puedo ir?
Turista B	Puede ir a la playa. Sitges no está muy lejos. Se puede ir en tren o en coche …

el puerto	*port*
el espectáculo	*entertainment, show*

Practice

1 During a holiday in a Spanish-speaking country you meet someone. How would you say the following? Use **poder** and **saber** as appropriate.

a Can you understand my Spanish?
b Can you speak more slowly? (**más despacio**)
c Can you repeat, please?
d Can you play tennis?
e I can't play today. We can play tomorrow.
f I can't drive. Can you drive?

2 Paco and Lucía are visiting Barcelona for the first time. Here's a conversation between them and the hotel receptionist. Change the infinitives in brackets into the appropriate form of the present tense.

Paco	Perdone, ¿(poder, nosotros) aparcar en esta calle?
Recepcionista	No, en esta calle no se (poder) aparcar. Pero (poder, Vds.) aparcar detrás del hotel.
Paco	Gracias. Por favor, ¿(poder, Vd.) recomendarnos un restaurante?
Recepcionista	(Poder, Vds.) comer en el restaurante del hotel. Está abierto.
Paco	Gracias. ¿Y dónde (poder, yo) hacer una llamada?
Recepcionista	Allí están los teléfonos, señor.

3 Label the signs below with the correct expression from the box.

> No entrar   No se puede nadar
> No hacer/tomar (L. Am.) fotografías
> No aparcar   No se puede girar/doblar a la izquierda
> No se puede fumar

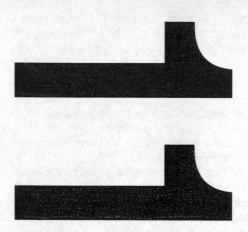

11

describing processes and procedures

In this unit you will learn how to
- describe processes and procedures
- ask questions regarding processes and procedures

Language points
- passive and active setence
- passive sentences with *ser* past participle
- passive sentences with *se*
- impersonal *tú*
- impersonal *ellos*

Key sentences

The main focus of this unit will be the language used in the description of processes and procedures. Ideas such as *The fruit is harvested and then packed and exported* or *Candidates are short-listed and then interviewed* can be expressed in Spanish in a variety of ways, as you will see from the examples and grammar notes which follow.

Describing processes and procedures

Las verduras se cortan, después se cocinan al vapor...

The vegetables are cut, then they are steamed...

La carne es procesada, y luego es embalada y exportada...

The meat is processed, and then packed and exported...

Asking questions regarding processes and procedures

¿Cómo se prepara una tortilla española?

How do you make a Spanish omelette?

¿Cómo se consigue/obtiene el permiso de trabajo/visado?

How do you get a work permit/visa?

Grammar summary

1 Passive and active sentences

Look at these sentences in English:

The farmers cut the oranges   *The oranges are cut by the farmers*

The first is an active sentence with an active verb: *the farmers cut the oranges*. The second sentence is passive: *the oranges are cut by the farmers*. In the passive sentence *the oranges* is the subject and *the farmers* is the agent carrying out the action expressed by the verb. In Spanish there are also active and passive sentences:

Los campesinos **cortan** las naranjas (active)

The farmers cut the oranges

Las naranjas **son cortadas por** los campesinos (passive)

The oranges are cut by the farmers

2 Passive sentences with *ser* + past participle

There are two main ways of forming passive sentences in Spanish. As in the last sentence, we may use the verb **ser** plus a past participle. The past participle is formed by adding the ending -**ado** to the stem of -**ar** verbs and -**ido** to the stem of -**er** and -**ir** verbs, for example:

cortar	Es cortado	*It's cut*
vender	Es vendido	*It's sold*
recibir	Es recibido	*It's received*

In this construction, the past participle will change for gender and number:

Las naranjas son cortadas	*The oranges are cut*
La fruta es vendida	*Fruit is sold*
Los productos son recibidos	*Products are received*

Irregular past participles

Some past participles are irregular. Here is a list of the most common ones:

abrir	*to open*	abierto
decir	*to say, tell*	dicho
escribir	*to write*	escrito
hacer	*to do, make*	hecho
poner	*to put*	puesto
romper	*to break*	roto
ver	*to see*	visto
volver	*to come back*	vuelto

Using passive sentences with *ser*

You should bear in mind the following points when using passive sentences with *ser*:

- The passive with **ser** is found more frequently in written and more formal language.

- The passive with **ser** is uncommon in the spoken language, particularly in Spain.

- If the agent of the action expressed by the verb is mentioned, use a passive with **ser** and not with **se**, e.g. las naranjas son cortadas **por** los campesinos.

- Some verbs do not allow the use of the passive with **ser** but, as there is no rule about it, only usage will tell you which ones cannot be used.

3 Passive sentences with *se*

In Unit 10 we studied the use of **se** with a 3rd person verb in impersonal sentences, e.g.:

Aquí no se puede aparcar   *One can't park here*

The same construction – **se** plus 3rd person verb – is used with a passive meaning, for example:

El libro **se** publicó en 1970   *The book was published in 1970*

Using passive sentences with *se*

You should bear in mind the following points when using passive sentences with **se**:

- The verb agrees in number (singular or plural) with the subject:

    Se fabrica aquí   *It's manufactured here*
    Se fabrican aquí   *They're manufactured here*

    Se produce en España   *It's produced in Spain*
    Se producen en España *They're produced in Spain*

- Passive sentences with **se** are not used when the agent of the action expressed by the verb is present. In such cases we must use a passive with **ser**:

    Los viajeros **son** recibidos **por** un guía ...   *Travellers are received by a guide ...*

- Generally speaking, passive sentences with **se** are more frequent than those with **ser**.

4 Impersonal *tú* (you) and *ellos* (they)

Processes and procedures may also be described using **tú** or **ellos** in an impersonal way:

Pides una solicitud de inscripción, la rellenas y la envías   *You ask for a registration form, you fill it in and send it*

Seleccionan a los mejores candidatos y los llaman para una entrevista   *They select the best candidates and they call them for an interview*

In context

1 Read these instructions on how to get a visa for a South American country.

Para obtener un visado de estudiante se debe ir personalmente al Consulado donde se rellena un formulario con los datos personales y los motivos del viaje. Se deben llevar tres fotografías tamaño pasaporte y una carta de la institución donde se va a estudiar. El visado debe ser solicitado por lo menos un mes antes de la fecha en que se piensa viajar. Para más información se puede llamar al teléfono 396 6907.

los datos personales	*personal information*
debe ser solicitado	*it must be requested*
por lo menos	*at least*
en que se piensa viajar	*when you're thinking of travelling*

2 Read this extract from a tourist brochure.

Los viajeros son recibidos en el aeropuerto por un guía y desde allí son trasladados a sus respectivos hoteles donde son atendidos por nuestro propio personal. Las excursiones son organizadas por agencias locales y se pueden pagar en moneda extranjera o moneda local ...

son trasladados	*they're transferred*
son atendidos	*they're looked after*
se pueden pagar	*they can be paid for*
en moneda extranjera	*in foreign currency*

Practice

1 Read this passage which describes the process for the selection of new staff in a Spanish company, and change each of the verb phrases in italics into the more colloquial third person plural of the verb.

Se estudian las solicitudes, *se realiza* una primera selección y *se invita* a los candidatos a participar en una serie de entrevistas, algunas de ellas de carácter informal. Luego de las entrevistas preliminares, *se hace* una segunda selección, en la que *se seleccionan* tres o cuatro candidatos. Después *se llama* a estos candidatos a una entrevista final, de carácter formal, y de entre ellos *se escoge* a una persona.

2 Rewrite these sentences changing the verbs and verb phrases in italics into the construction of **se** + third person of the verb.

a Primero *cortas* la cebolla muy fina y la *fríes* durante unos minutos. Luego le *pones* un poco de vino.

b La fruta *es seleccionada*, y luego *es llevada* hasta los puertos y desde allí *es enviada* al exterior.

c Los hoteles *son elegidos* cuidadosamente y *son evaluados* periódicamente.

12

expressing wants and preferences

In this unit you will learn how to

- ask and answer questions about wants
- ask and answer questions about preferences

Language points

- *querer* + noun/pronoun/v
- *preferir* + noun/pronoun/v
- direct object pronouns
- personal *a*
- other verbs expressing w

Key sentences

In this unit dealing with wants and preferences you will learn the use of verbs such as **querer**, *to want*, and **preferir**, *to prefer*, and the Spanish equivalent of words such as *me, you, him, her*.

Asking and answering questions about wants

¿Qué quieres/quiere Vd.?	*What do you want?*
Quiero una camisa/un vestido	*I want a shirt/dress*
Quiero (ver) ésta/éste	*I want (to see) this one*

Asking and answering questions about preferences

¿Cuál prefieres/prefiere Vd.?	*Which one do you prefer?*
Prefiero el azul/negro	*I prefer the blue/black one*
Prefiero (comprar/llevar) ése	*I prefer (to buy/take) that one*

Grammar summary

1 *Querer* + noun/pronoun/verb

Querer (e → ie) is the verb most frequently used in Spanish to ask and answer questions about wants. It may be used with a noun, a pronoun or a verb.

A noun

Quiero **un zumo/jugo de naranja**	*I want an orange juice*
Queremos **una habitación**	*We want a room*

A pronoun

¿Quieres **algo**?	*Do you want something?*
Quiero **esto**	*I want this*

A verb

Quiero **alquilar** un coche	*I want to hire a car*
Queremos **ir** al teatro	*We want to go to the theatre*

2 *Preferir* + noun/pronoun/verb

Preferir (e → ie) is the verb most frequently used in Spanish to ask and answer questions about preferences. It may be used with a noun, a pronoun or a verb.

A noun

Prefiero **el tenis**	*I prefer tennis*
Él prefiere **el fútbol**	*He prefers football*

A pronoun

Prefiero **éste**	*I prefer this one*
Prefiero pescado. ¿Cómo **lo** prefiere? **Lo** prefiero a la plancha	*I prefer fish. How do you prefer it? I prefer it grilled*

A verb

Preferimos **ir** a Mallorca	*We prefer to go to Mallorca*
Prefieren **quedarse** en casa	*They prefer to stay at home*
Luis prefiere **aprender** inglés	*Luis prefers to learn English*

3 Direct object pronouns

1st and 2nd person

Words such as *me, you, him, her, it*, etc., as in *He prefers me, I prefer you* and *I don't want it*, are called direct object pronouns. Object pronouns for the 1st and 2nd person singular are:

		Singular	
me	*me*	**Me** prefiere	*He prefers me*
te	*you* (fam.)	**Te** prefiere	*He prefers you*
		Plural	
nos	*us*	**Nos** prefiere	*He prefers us*
os	*you* (fam.)	**Os** prefiere	*He prefers you*

3rd person

Now look at these examples and explanations regarding the use of 3rd person object pronouns:

¿Cómo quiere el pescado?	*How do you want the fish?*
Lo quiero frito	*I want it fried*
¿Cómo quiere las patatas?	*How do you want the potatoes?*
Las quiero fritas	*I want them fried*

In order to avoid the repetition of the nouns **el pescado** and **las patatas** we have used instead the pronoun **lo** (masculine, singular) and **las** (feminine, plural). **Lo** and **las** are direct object pronouns. **Lo** refers back to the object **el pescado** and **las** refers back to **las patatas**. Direct object pronouns agree in gender and number with the noun they refer to. Here are the 3rd person forms:

lo (masc. sing.)	los (masc. pl.)
la (fem. sing)	las (fem. pl.)

Direct object pronouns can refer to people

In the following sentences 3rd person object pronouns refer to people rather than things:

Prefiero a Carmen	*I prefer Carmen*
La prefiero	*I prefer her*
Prefiero a Carmen y Elena	*I prefer Carmen and Elena*
Las prefiero	*I prefer them*

Carmen, in the first sentence, and Carmen and Elena in the second sentence, are direct objects replaced by **la** (fem. sing.) and **las** (fem. pl.) respectively. The use of **la** and **las** for a human female direct object seems to present no variation throughout the Spanish-speaking world. However, when it comes to human male direct objects there are two main dialectal differences.

¿*Le* or *lo*?

In the Spanish-speaking countries of Latin America as well as in some parts of non-central Spain you will hear **lo** (singular) and **los** (plural) used for males, as for things. In Madrid and in some regions of central Spain in general, you are much more likely to hear **le** (singular) and **les** (plural) used for human males and **lo** (singular) and **los** (plural) used for things. Both usages are correct but the latter may be easier for you to remember. Here are some examples:

Yo **lo** prefiero	*I prefer him/it*
Yo **le** prefiero	*I prefer him*
Ella **lo** quiere	*She loves him/it*
Ella **le** quiere	*She loves him*

Direct address

In direct address **lo** (**le**) – **la** and **los** (**les**) – **las** stand for **usted** and **ustedes** respectively, for example:

Ellos **lo** (**le**) prefieren	*They prefer you* (masc. sing.)
Yo **la** quiero aquí	*I want you here* (fem. sing.)

Position of direct object pronouns

The normal position of the object pronoun is before the main verb, as shown in the previous examples. However, in phrases where a verb precedes an infinitive or a gerund, the object pronoun may either precede the main verb or be attached to the infinitive or gerund:

Quiero hacerlo	*I want to do it*
Lo quiero hacer	*I want to do it*
Estoy terminándolo	*I'm finishing it.*
Lo estoy terminando.	*I'm finishing it.*

Direct object pronouns precede negative imperatives but are attached to positive forms.

| No lo haga. | *Don't do it.* |
| Hágalo. | *Do it.* |

(For the imperative see Unit 20.)

4 Personal *a*

Observe these sentences:

| Prefiero a Carmen | *I prefer Carmen* |
| Quiero a Juan | *I love Juan* |

A peculiarity of Spanish is that the preposition **a** is placed before a direct object if the object is a definite person. This use of the preposition **a** is known as 'personal **a**'.

5 Other verbs expressing wants

Desear

Desear, literally *to wish*, is used in more formal contexts and is much less frequent than **querer**:

¿Desea Vd. algo?	*Would you like anything?*
¿Qué desea?	*What would you like?*
	(in a shop, office, etc.)

Quisiera

Quisiera, *I would like*, from **querer**, is used in place of **quiero** or **queremos** to add more politeness to a request:

| Quisiera una habitación | *I'd like a room* |
| Quisiéramos hablar con Vd. | *We'd like to speak to you* |

In context

1 In a restaurant.

| **Camarero** | ¿Qué van a tomar? |
| **Roberto** | Yo quiero sopa de verduras y de segundo pescado con ensalada. |

Camarero	El pescado, ¿cómo lo quiere? Frito, a la plancha...
Roberto	Lo prefiero a la plancha.
Camarero	¿Y usted señor?
Juan	Para mí una tortilla de patatas y de segundo quiero chuletas de cerdo.
Camarero	Las chuletas, ¿con qué las quiere?
Juan	Con puré.
Camarero	¿Y para beber?
Roberto	Una botella de vino de la casa.
Camarero	¿Prefieren blanco o tinto?
Roberto	Tinto.
Camarero	De acuerdo. Un momento, por favor.

la sopa de verduras	vegetable soup
de segundo	as a second course
el vino de la casa	house wine
blanco o tinto	white or red
de acuerdo	all right

2 Buying a shirt.

Dependienta	Buenas tardes. ¿Qué desea?
Elisa	Quiero una camisa de ésas. ¿Cuánto valen?
Dependienta	Éstas las tenemos de oferta a 25 euros. ¿De qué color la quiere?
Elisa	La prefiero en azul.
Dependienta	¿Qué talla tiene?
Elisa	Treinta y ocho.
Dependienta	Aquí tiene Vd. una en azul.
Elisa	Sí, está muy bien. ¿Puedo probármela?
Dependienta	Sí, por supuesto. Pase por aquí, por favor.

¿qué desea?	what would you like?
¿cuánto valen?	how much are they?
de oferta	special offer
¿puedo probármela?	may I try it on?
por supuesto	certainly
pase por aquí	come this way

Notice the use of direct object pronouns in the following sentences from dialogue 1:

El pescado, ¿cómo lo quiere? Lo refers back to el pescado.
Las chuletas, ¿con qué las quiere? Las refers back to las chuletas.

Note also the question ¿**Puedo probármela?** *May I try it on?*

The verb here is **probarse** (*to try on*), a reflexive verb. Both the reflexive pronoun **me** and the direct object pronoun **la** (which refers back to **la camisa**) have been added to the infinitive. An alternative position would be: ¿**me la** puedo probar?

Practice

1 You and a travelling companion are booking into a hotel in a Spanish-speaking country. Fill in your part of the conversation with the hotel receptionist.

Recepcionista	Buenas tardes. ¿Qué desean?
Tú	*Say you'd like a double room. Ask if they have any.*
Recepcionista	¿Prefieren una interior o exterior?
Tú	*Say you prefer one facing the street, but you'd like to see it. Ask if it is possible.*
Recepcionista	Sí, por supuesto. Pasen por aquí, por favor.
Tú	*Say it's all right, you want to take the room, but you'd like to know what it costs.*
Recepcionista	Quince mil pesos con desayuno y veinte mil con media pensión.
Tú	*Say you want the room only. You prefer to eat out* (fuera).
Recepcionista	De acuerdo.

2 Can you make sense of these exchanges between customers and a waiter in a restaurant? Match each request with an appropriate question or statement.

a Quiero pollo, por favor.
b Para mí, patatas/papas (L.Am.).
c Dos cafés, por favor.
d Por favor, la cuenta.

1 Un momento por favor, ahora mismo los traigo.
2 ¿Con qué lo quiere?
3 Aquí la tiene.
4 ¿Cómo las quiere?

3 Complete the speech bubbles with a suitable phrase, according to the item being bought: una muñeca (*a doll*), un sombrero (*a hat*), una chaqueta (*a jacket*), unas gafas de sol (*sunglasses*).

a Prefiero el blanco.
b Quiero ésta. La otra es demasiado pequeña.
c Prefiero ésta, la más pequeña.
d Quiero unas más pequeñas. Éstas son muy grandes.
e Quiero éste, el más pequeño.
f Éstos son demasiado pequeños. Prefiero unos más grandes.

13

expressing likes and dislikes

In this unit you will learn how to
- say whether you like or dislike something
- give similar information about other people
- ask questions about likes and dislikes

Language points
- *gustar*
- indirect object pronouns
- prepositional forms of pronouns
- position of indirect object pronouns
- other verbs expressing likes and dislikes

Key sentences

In the grammar notes that follow you will find information about how to express likes and dislikes using the verb **gustar**, *to like*. You will also find an explanation of the pronouns which are normally used with this verb.

Saying whether you like or dislike something

Me/nos **gusta** el tenis/nadar   *I/we like tennis/swimming*
No me/nos **gusta** esa música/   *We don't like that music/*
   ver la televisión   *watching television*

Saying whether others like or dislike something

Le **gusta** España/**gustan** los   *He/she likes Spain/*
   españoles   *Spaniards*
Te **gusta/gustan**, ¿verdad?   *You like it/them, don't you?*
A Sol y Paco/ellos les **gusta**   *Sol and Paco/they like dancing*
   bailar

Asking questions about likes and dislikes

¿Te/le **gusta** el español?   *Do you like Spanish?*
                             (fam./pol.)
¿Qué os/les **gusta** hacer?   *What do you like doing?*
                             (fam./pol.)

Grammar summary

1 *Gustar*

To say whether you like or dislike something you can use the verb **gustar**. It is a special kind of verb which is normally used in the 3rd person singular or plural, depending on the number of the noun which follows. The verb must be preceded by an indirect object pronoun. These are words such as **me** (*me, to me*), **te** (*you, to you*), as in **me gusta** (*I like it*, or, literally, *it is pleasing to me*), **te gusta** (*you like it* or, literally, *it is pleasing to you*). An explanation about indirect object pronouns is necessary before giving further examples of the use of **gustar**.

2 Indirect object pronouns

In Unit 12 we studied direct object pronouns, as found in sentences like **lo quiero** (*I want it*), **los quiero** (*I want them*), **me prefiere** (*he/she prefers me*). Here we are dealing with another set of pronouns – indirect object pronouns – which, although mostly similar in form to the others, are used differently.

1st and 2nd person indirect object pronouns

Consider this sentence:

El recepcionista me cambia   *The receptionist changes the*
    el dinero   *money for me*

Here, the subject of the sentence is **el recepcionista** (*the receptionist*), the direct object is **el dinero** (*the money*, the thing changed) and the indirect object is **me** (*for me*, that is, the person for whom the money is changed). First and 2nd person indirect object pronouns are no different in form from direct object pronouns (see page 84). Here are their forms:

Subject pronouns		Indirect object pronouns	
yo	*I*	me	*me, to me, for me*
tú	*you* (fam. sing.)	te	*you, to you, for you*
nosotros/as	*we*	nos	*us, to us, for us*
vosotros/as	*you* (fam. pl.)	os	*you, to you, for you*

In sentences with **gustar**, indirect object pronouns will translate literally as *to me, to you, to us*:

me gusta	*I like it* (lit. *it is pleasing to me*)
te gusta	*you like it* (lit. *it is pleasing to you*)
nos gusta	*we like it* (lit. *it is pleasing to us*)
os gusta	*you like it* (lit. *it is pleasing to you*)

The verb itself may be in the plural:

me gustan	*I like them* (lit. *they're pleasing to me*)
te gustan	*you like them* (lit. *they're pleasing to you*)
no nos gustan	*we don't like them* (lit. *they're not pleasing to us*)

Notice that negative senteces are formed by placing **no** before the pronoun.

Here are some examples of the use of indirect object pronouns with verbs other than **gustar**:

¿Me/nos da el dinero,   *Will you give me/us the*
    por favor?   *money, please?*

¿Te traigo el periódico?	*Shall I bring you the newspaper?*
Él me/nos enseña español	*He teaches me/us Spanish*

3rd person indirect object pronouns

In the 3rd person, the indirect object pronoun is **le** for both masculine and feminine. The plural form is **les**:

Subject pronouns		Indirect object pronouns	
usted	*you* (pol.)	le	*you, to you, for you*
él	*he*	le	*him, to him, for him*
ella	*she*	le	*her, to her, for her*
ustedes	*you* (pol.)	les	*you, to you, for you*
ellos/as	*they*	les	*them, to them, for them*

Here are some examples with **gustar**:

Le gusta viajar	*You like/he/she/likes to travel*
Les gusta España	*You/they like Spain*
¿Le gusta el vino español?	*Do you/does he/she like Spanish wine?*

Here are some examples with verbs other than **gustar**:

¿Le doy el pasaporte?	*Shall I give you/him/her the passport?*
Ella le prepara la cena	*She prepares dinner for you/him/her*
Él les repara el coche	*He repairs the car for you/them*

3 Prepositional forms of pronouns

Consider this sentence from the previous examples: **Le gusta viajar**. This sentence translates into English in three different ways: *You like to travel, he likes to travel, she likes to travel.* To avoid this kind of ambiguity, and also to add emphasis, we use another set of pronouns preceded by the preposition **a**:

A usted le gusta viajar	*You like to travel*
A él le gusta viajar	*He likes to travel*
A ella le gusta viajar	*She likes to travel*

For the plural we use **a ustedes, a ellos, a ellas**:

A ustedes les gusta España	*You like Spain*
A ellos les gusta Madrid	*They like Madrid* (masc.)
A ellas les gusta Sevilla	*They like Seville* (fem.)

Notice also:

A **Alfonso** no le gusta fumar	*Alfonso doesn't like to smoke*
A **Cristina** no le gusta beber	*Christina doesn't like to drink*
A **Luis y Juan** no les gusta esto	*Luis and Juan don't like this*

Emphatic use of prepositional pronouns

Sometimes the function of prepositional pronouns is purely emphatic:

A **mí** me gusta	*I like it*
A **ti** te gusta	*you like it*
A **nosotros** nos gusta	*we like it*
A **vosotros** os gusta	*you like it*

4 Position of indirect object pronouns

The position of indirect object pronouns is the same as that of direct object pronouns, that is, normally before the main verb. But when there are two object pronouns in a sentence (which may happen with verbs other than **gusta**), one indirect and one direct, the indirect object pronoun must come first. Consider these sentences:

Él me cambia el dinero	*He changes the money for me*
Él me lo cambia	*He changes it for me*

When the indirect object **le** or **les** precedes **lo**, **la**, **los** or **las**, the indirect object becomes **se**:

Yo le cambio el dinero	*I change the money for you*
Yo lo cambio	*I change it*
Yo se lo cambio	*I change it for you*

5   Other verbs expressing likes and dislikes

Verbs such as **encantar**, **fascinar** (*to like very much*, *to love*), and **agradar** (*to like*) function in the same way as **gustar**.

Nos **encanta** hablar español.	*We love to speak Spanish*
Me **fascina** Sevilla	*I love Seville*
No le **agradan** las fiestas	*He/she doesn't like parties*

Agradar is less frequent and less colloquial than **gustar**.

In context

1 In Seville for the first time.

Ella ¿Te gusta Sevilla?
Él Sí, me gusta muchísimo. ¿Y a ti?
Ella A mí también, pero hace mucho calor, ¿verdad?
Él Sí, yo prefiero el clima de Galicia.
Ella A mí no me gusta nada la lluvia. En Galicia llueve demasiado.

la lluvia	*rain*
llueve demasiado	*it rains too much*

2 An interview about Madrid.

Periodista Señor, ¿le gusta a Vd. Madrid?
Señor Sí y no.
Periodista ¿Qué es lo que le gusta de Madrid?
Señor Me gustan sus museos, sus espectáculos, sus restaurantes que son estupendos ...
Periodista ¿Y qué es lo que no le gusta?
Señor Bueno, no me gusta el tráfico excesivo que tiene Madrid. Es una ciudad muy ruidosa y a mí me gusta la tranquilidad.

To avoid repetition of the same verb, in this case **gustar**, we use the construction **a** + prepositional pronoun. Observe these phrases from dialogue 1:

Sí, me gusta muchísimo. ¿Y **a ti?**	*Yes, I like it very much. Do you?*
A mí también	*I do too*

The same construction may be used in negative sentences with **tampoco:**

No me gusta Madrid. ¿Y **a usted?**	*I don't like Madrid. Do you?*
A mí tampoco	*I don't either*

Practice

1 Fill in the blank spaces in these sentences with a suitable pronoun.

a A Juan no ... gusta el fútbol.
b A nosotros ... gusta hacer deportes.

c A Carmen y Antonio ... gusta mucho viajar.
d A ... me gustan los idiomas.
e A ... también te gustan, ¿verdad?
f A ella ... encanta el cine.
g Y a vosotros, ¿qué ... gusta hacer en las vacaciones?
h A mí y a mi familia ... encantan los españoles.

2 You are thinking of sharing your place with a Spanish-speaking person, so you want to know what he/she likes or dislikes. How would you ask him/her the following?

a Whether he/she likes the room.
b Whether he/she likes to cook.
c What music he/she likes.
d What television programmes he/she likes (**programas de televisión**).
e Whether he/she likes animals (**los animales**).
f What he/she likes to do at weekends (**los fines de semana**).

3 Can you say what these people like to do on their holidays? Match the pictures with the phrases below and write full sentences using **gustar**. Follow the example:

Enrique – leer y escuchar música
A Enrique le gusta leer y escuchar música.

1 Rafael y su novia – ir de camping
2 Juan – levantarse tarde
3 Andrés – montar en bicicleta
4 Ángeles – descansar y tomar el sol
5 Paco – nadar
6 María y su familia – ir de vacaciones a Nueva York

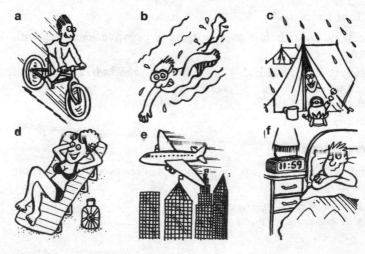

asking and giving opinions

In this unit you will learn how to
- ask opinions
- give opinions

Language points
- *parecer*
- relative pronoun *que*
- other verbs used in expressing opinions
- phrases expressing opinions

Key sentences

As in English, opinions in Spanish can be expressed in a variety of ways, using verbs like **parecer**, *to seem*, **pensar, creer, opinar**, *to think*, or expressions such as **a mi parecer, en mi opinión**, *in my opinion*.

Asking someone's opinion

¿Qué te parece el hotel/ la gente? — *What do you think of the hotel/the people?*

¿Qué opinas/piensas de él? — *What do you think about him?*

¿No crees que tengo razón? — *Don't you think I'm right?*

Giving opinions

Me parecen guapos/ simpáticos — *I think they are good-looking/ nice*

Lo considero difícil/ imposible — *I believe it's difficult/ impossible*

Creo/pienso que es una buena idea — *I think it's a good idea*

Grammar study

1 *Parecer* (to think, seem)

To ask and give opinions we can use **parecer**, a 2nd conjugation verb which in this context functions grammatically like **gustar**, that is, it is used in the 3rd person singular or plural and it is preceded by an indirect object pronoun:

¿Qué **te parece** San Sebastián? — *What do you think of San Sebastián?*

Me parece una ciudad muy bonita — *I think it's a very nice city*

Literally, these last two sentences would translate as: *What does San Sebastián seem to you? It seems a very nice city to me.* Likewise:

¿Qué **os parecen** estas playas? — *What do you think of those beaches?*
(What do these beaches seem to you?)

| Nos **parecen** muy contaminadas | *We think they're very polluted (They seem very polluted to us)* |

2 *Que* (that, which, who)

The word *that*, as in *I think that it's a good idea*, translates into Spanish as **que**. In English the word may be omitted, but not, however, in Spanish. Consider the use of **que** and its English equivalent in the following examples:

Creo **que** ella tiene razón	*I think (that) she's right*
El último libro **que** escribió es muy bueno	*The last book (which) he/she wrote is very good*
La persona **que** llamó me pareció muy agradable	*The person who phoned seemed very pleasant*

For more information on this see **Relative pronouns** on page 183 of the **Grammar reference**.

3 Other verbs used in the expression of opinions

Here are some other verbs used in the expression of opinions.

pensar (e → ie) (to think)

¿Qué **piensa** Vd. de mí?	*What do you think of me?*
Pienso que es Vd. muy amable	*I think you're very kind*
Pensamos que es una idea excelente	*We think it's an excellent idea*

creer (to think)

¿Qué **cree** Vd. que puede pasar?	*What do you think can happen?*
Creo que no hay que preocuparse	*I don't think one needs to worry*
Creo que sí/no	*I think so/don't think so*

opinar (to think)

| ¿Qué **opinan** Vds. de lo que digo? | *What do you think of what I'm saying?* |
| Yo **opino** que Vd. tiene razón | *I think you're right* |

considerar (to consider, think)

| **Considero** que debemos hablar con él | *I think we should speak to him* |
| Ella **considera** que es suficiente | *She thinks it's enough* |

4 Phrases expressing opinions

Personal opinions may also be expressed using phrases such as
a mi parecer, a mi juicio, en mi opinión, all of which mean *in
my opinion*.

A mi parecer no debemos aceptar	*In my opinion we mustn't accept*
A mi juicio, ella es la persona más apropiada	*In my opinion, she is the most suitable person*
En mi opinión, debemos decírselo	*In my opinion, we must tell him/her*

In context

Javier and Eva have just met at the lounge of their hotel in
Spain. They discuss the place where they're staying.

Javier ¿Qué te parece el hotel?

Eva Creo que no está nada mal, aunque la comida no me parece muy buena.

Javier Las habitaciones son estupendas, ¿no crees tú?

Eva Bueno, sí, la mía tiene una vista fantástica, pero es un poco ruidosa. ¿Y la ciudad te gusta?

Javier Sí, pienso que está bien, pero hay demasiada gente. Prefiero los sitios pequeños.

Eva Sí, yo también.

Javier ¿Estás libre ahora?

Eva Sí. No tengo nada que hacer.

Javier ¿Qué te parece si vamos a tomar un café?

Eva De acuerdo. Vamos.

no está nada mal	*it's not bad at all*
el sitio	*place*
¿qué te parece si vamos...?	*What about going...?*
vamos	*let's go*

Notice the use of the word **aunque** (*although*) in the following
sentence from the dialogue:

Creo que no está nada mal, **aunque** la comida no me parece muy buena	*I don't think it's bad at all, although I don't think the food is very good*

Aunque is normally used when we wish to establish a contrast
between two ideas.

Practice

1 A Spanish-speaking friend is visiting you at home for the first time, so you want to know what he/she thinks of the place and the people. Ask his/her opinion about the following using the expressions in brackets.

a La ciudad (parecer)   **d** La gente (pensar)
b Los museos (parecer)   **e** Mis amigos (opinar)
c Los parques (opinar)   **f** La vida en la ciudad (pensar)

2 Antonio, from Spain, is spending some time with his relatives in Buenos Aires, the capital of Argentina. In a letter to you, he gives his opinion about the place. Fill in the gaps in this passage with an appropriate expression from the list, without repeating any.

> a mi parecer   en mi opinión   parecer
> considerar   creer   pensar

No te imaginas lo que es esta ciudad. A mí me (1)... fantástica y (2)... que los argentinos son muy simpáticos. (3)..., lo mejor de esta ciudad es la vida nocturna y la vida cultural. La vida cultural, especialmente, la (4)... excelente. Hay mucho que ver. La ciudad es agradable, aunque, (5)..., la vida aquí no es fácil. (6)... que es una ciudad muy cara.

3 You are on holiday in a Spanish-speaking country. A Spanish-speaking friend phones you at your hotel. Follow the guidelines and fill in your part of the conversation.

Tu amigo/a   ¿Qué te parece el hotel?
Tú   *Say you think the hotel is very good, but you think the people are a bit noisy.*
Tu amigo/a   Y la playa, ¿qué tal?
Tú   *Say you think the beach is excellent.*
Tu amigo/a   Sí, es una playa muy buena. ¿Estás libre esta noche?
Tú   *Say yes, you are free, and ask your friend what he/she thinks about going to a disco* (una disco).
Tu amigo/a   De acuerdo, vamos. Podemos ir a la disco que está cerca del hotel. ¿No te parece?

15 referring to future plans and events

In this unit you will learn how to

- ask and answer questions about future plans
- ask and answer questions about future events

Language points

- *ir a* + infinitive
- future tense
- present tense with future meaning
- *pensar* to refer to plans and intentions
- the future of probability

Key sentences

As in English, future plans and future events can be expressed in Spanish in a number of ways, the future tense being only one of them.

Look at the examples and grammar notes that follow to find out how to use the Spanish equivalent of sentences such as *I am going to do it, What time will the meeting be?*

Asking and answering questions about future plans

¿Vas/vais a hacerlo/comprarlo? *Are you going to do/buy it?*
Voy/vamos a hacerlo/comprarlo *I'm/we're going to do/buy it*

Asking and answering questions about future events

¿A qué hora será/empezará   *What time will the meeting be/*
la reunión?   *begin?*
No tendremos/haremos   *We won't have/hold the*
la reunión   *meeting*

Grammar summary

1 *Ir a* + infinitive

Future plans and intentions are normally expressed with the present tense of **ir** (**voy, vas, va, vamos, vais, van**) followed by the preposition **a** and an infinitive. This construction is equivalent to the English *to be going to* + infinitive. It is popular in Spanish and it is often used to replace the future tense. Here are some examples:

¿Qué **vas a** hacer esta   *What are you going to do*
noche?   *tonight?*
Voy a salir a cenar   *I'm going out for dinner*
¿Cuándo **vais a** volver?   *When are you going to return?*
Vamos a volver el sábado *We're going to return on*
                              Saturday

2 Future tense

Uses

The future tense has become less common in the spoken language where it is being gradually replaced by the construction explained earlier. Nowadays its use is restricted more to certain contexts. In formal written language such as that of the press, for instance, the future tense is very frequent. In spoken language it is often used in sentences expressing promises, commands and a certain degree of uncertainty.

Formation

To form the future tense you use the infinitive followed by the ending, which is the same for the three conjugations. Here are the future forms of three regular verbs representing each of the three conjugations:

estar (*to be*)		**ver** (*to see*)	
estaré	*I will be*	veré	*I will see*
estarás	*you will be* (fam.)	verás	*you will see* (fam.)
estará	*you/he/she will be*	verá	*you/he/she will see*
estaremos	*we will be*	veremos	*we will see*
estaréis	*you will be* (fam.)	veréis	*you will see* (fam.)
estarán	*you/they will be*	verán	*you/they will see*
		ir (*to go*)	
iré	*I will go*	iremos	*we will go*
irás	*you will go* (fam.)	iréis	*you will go* (fam.)
irá	*you/he/she will go*	irán	*you/they will go*

Press language:

El presidente de Venezuela llegará a Barajas a las 7.30 horas, donde será recibido por el presidente del gobierno español.

The president of Venezuela will arrive at Barajas at 7.30, where he will be received by the president of the Spanish government.

La nueva fábrica de automóviles que se instalará en Zaragoza iniciará su producción el 30 de junio próximo.

The new car factory which will be installed in Zaragoza will start production on 30 June.

Expressing promises:

Te lo daré mañana   *I'll give it to you tomorrow*
No se lo contaré   *I won't tell him*

Expressing commands:
Os quedaréis aquí   *You'll stay here*
Lo terminarás inmediatemente *You'll finish it immediately*

Expressing a degree of uncertainty:
Irás a Francia, ¿verdad?   *You'll go to France, won't*
                                         you?

Me ayudarás, ¿no?   *You will help me, won't you?*

Irregular future forms
Some verbs have an irregular stem in the future tense but the
endings are the same as those of regular verbs. Here is a list of
the most important:

decir (*to say, tell*)	diré, dirás, dirá, diremos, diréis, dirán
haber (*to have*, auxiliary)	habré, habrás, habrá habremos, habréis, habrán
hacer (*to do, make*)	haré, harás, hará, haremos, haréis, harán
obtener (*to obtain*)	obtendré, obtendrás, obtendrá, obtendremos, obtendréis, obtendrán
poder (*can, be able to*)	podré, podrás, podrá, podremos, podréis, podrán
poner (*to put*)	pondré, pondrás, pondrá, pondremos, pondréis, pondrán
querer (*to want*)	querré, querrás, querrá, querremos, querréis, querrán
saber (*to know*)	sabré, sabrás, sabrá, sabremos, sabréis, sabrán
salir (*to go out*)	saldré, saldrás, saldrá, saldremos, saldréis, saldrán
tener (*to have*)	tendré, tendrás, tendrá, tendremos, tendréis, tendrán
venir (*to come*)	vendré, vendrás, vendrá, vendremos, vendréis, vendrán

For a list of the most common irregular verbs see pages 203–6.

¿Qué harás mañana?	*What will you do tomorrow?*
Saldré con Ana	*I'll go out with Ana*
Tendrás que decírmelo	*You'll have to tell me*
No te lo diré	*I won't tell you*

Podrá Vd. venir el lunes, ¿verdad?	*You'll be able to come on Monday, won't you?*
Creo que no podré	*I don't think I'll be able to*

3 Present tense with future meaning

As in English, Spanish also uses the present tense to refer to the future, particularly to the immediate future and with verbs which indicate movement (e.g. **ir**, *to go*; **salir**, *to go out*; **venir**, *to come*), but also with the verb **hacer** (*to do*). Time phrases such as **mañana** (*tomorrow*), **pasado mañana** (*the day after tomorrow*), **la semana que viene** (*next week*), **el mes que viene** (*next month*), **la semana próxima** (*next week*), **el mes próximo** (*next month*), etc., will make it clear that the time reference is the future and not the present. Here are some examples:

¿Qué haces **mañana**?	*What are you doing tomorrow?*
Voy a la piscina	*I'm going to the swimming pool*
Salimos pasado mañana	*We leave the day after tomorrow*
Él **llega** la **semana que viene**	*He is arriving next week*

4 *Pensar* to refer to plans and intentions

Pensar (*to think, to be thinking of*) is often used to refer to future plans and intentions in sentences like these:

¿Qué **piensas** hacer este verano?	*What are you thinking of doing this summer?*
Pienso ir a Nueva York	*I'm thinking of going to New York*
Pensamos casarnos	*We're thinking of getting married*

5 The future of probability

The future tense is often used to express probability or conjecture in sentences like these:

¿Qué hora **será**?	*I wonder what time it is?/ what time can it be?*
Serán las dos	*It must be 2 o'clock*
¿Dónde **estará** María?	*I wonder where María is/ where can María be?*

In context

1 Víctor and Mercedes talk about their summer holiday.

Víctor	¿Qué vais a hacer tú y Pablo este verano?
Mercedes	Vamos a ir a Buenos Aires a visitar a unos parientes.
Víctor	¿Vais con los chicos?
Mercedes	No, ellos van a quedarse con los abuelos en Madrid.
Víctor	¿Cuánto tiempo vais a estar allí?
Mercedes	Un mes solamente. Vamos a volver a finales de agosto. ¿Y tú qué planes tienes? ¿Irás otra vez a Málaga?
Víctor	No, esta vez iré a casa de unos amigos en Ibiza.
Mercedes	Ibiza te gustará mucho. Es un lugar precioso. ¿Vas a quedarte mucho tiempo?
Víctor	Un par de semanas. Tendré que volver antes del quince pues viene Marta a pasar unos días conmigo ...

a finales de	*at the end of*
otra vez	*again*
esta vez	*this time*
un par de semanas	*a couple of weeks*
a pasar unos días	*to spend some days*

2 Read this paragraph from a newspaper.

El 1 de abril próximo llegará a nuestro país en visita oficial el ministro de asuntos exteriores británico Sir John Perkins, quien se entrevistará con el jefe del gobierno español. El ministro permanecerá en Madrid por espacio de tres días y en las conversaciones que sostendrá con las autoridades de gobierno se tratará el tema de Gibraltar ...

el ministro de asuntos exteriores	*minister of foreign affairs*
entrevistarse	*to meet*
por espacio de	*for, during*
permanecer	*to remain*
sostener	*to hold*
tratar	*to deal with*

Practice

1 Here are Miguel's and María and Alberto's plans for this summer.

Miguel	María and Alberto
Hacer un curso de inglés en Inglaterra	Viajar a la India

a How would you ask Miguel what he's going to do this summer and how would you ask María and Alberto the same question?

b How would Miguel reply? And María and Alberto?

c How would you tell someone else about their plans?

d How would you tell someone what *you* are going to do?

2 Sara wrote to Ana announcing her travel plans. Change the infinitives in brackets into the appropriate form of the future tense.

Querida Ana

Te escribo para confirmarte mi viaje a Madrid, que (1) (ser) el sábado 15 de septiembre. (2) (Salir, yo) de aquí a las 9.00 de la mañana y (3) (llegar) al aeropuerto de Barajas a las 12.00. (4) (Quedarse) en el hotel Victoria, y te (5) (llamar) inmediatamente. No (6) (poder) estar más de dos días en Madrid, porque (7) (tener) que viajar a Andalucía, pero en esos dos días (8) (poder, nosotras) salir juntas. (9) (Venir, tú) conmigo a Toledo, ¿verdad? (10) (Tener, tú) que acompañarme.

3 What will Ana do next year? Match the drawings with the phrases below and write full sentences using the correct form of the future tense.

a (Ir) de vacaciones a Londres.

b (Hacer) un curso de inglés.

c (Practicar) deportes.

d (Estudiar) enfermería.

16 making requests and offers

In this unit you will learn how to
- make requests
- reply to a request
- make offers
- reply to offers

Language points
- present tense in requests and offers
- *poder* and *querer* in requests and offers
- *podría* in requests

Key sentences

We can make requests and offers in English in a number of ways. Consider for instance the following sentences: *Will you help me, please?*, *Can you show me the way?*, *Shall I carry your suitcase?*, *Can I make you some coffee?* and *Do you want some biscuits?* Spanish too, has several ways of expressing these ideas. The examples and notes that follow will teach you how to construct sentences of this type using some of the grammar you learned in previous units.

Making requests

¿Me/nos trae más pan, por favor?	*Will you bring me/us some more bread, please?*
¿Puedes ayudarme/nos?	*Can you help me/us?*

Replying to a request

Por supuesto/Desde luego	*Of course/Certainly*
Naturalmente/Con mucho gusto	*Certainly/With pleasure*

Making offers

¿Le/te llevo la maleta?	*Shall I carry your suitcase?*
¿Quieres/desea un café?	*Do you want/Would you like some coffee?*

Replying to offers

Sí/Bueno/De acuerdo, (muchas) gracias	*Yes/All right, thank you (very much)*
Vale, gracias	*Okay, thank you*
(Es Vd.) muy amable	*That's very kind*

Grammar summary

1 Present tense in requests and offers

Requests

A frequent way of making requests is by using the present tense preceded by an object pronoun, for example:

¿Me despierta a las 7.00, por favor?	*Will you wake me at 7.00 please?*
¿Me pasa la sal?	*Will you pass the salt?*
¿Nos llama un taxi?	*Will you call a taxi for us?*
¿Le dice a Gloria que estoy aquí, por favor?	*Will you tell Gloria I'm here, please?*

Offers

The same construction – present tense preceded by an object pronoun – may be used in making offers. Here are some examples:

¿Le doy un poco más?	*Shall I give you some more?*
¿Les reservo una habitación?	*Shall I book a room for you?*
¿Te ayudo?	*Shall I help you?*
¿Os llamo a las 6.00?	*Shall I call you at 6.00?*

2 *Poder* in requests and offers

Requests

Poder (*can, be able to*) is used in requests in sentences like these:

¿**Puede** llamar al Sr. Martínez, por favor?	*Can you call señor Martínez, please?*
¿**Pueden** darnos otra mesa, por favor?	*Can you give us another table, please?*
¿**Puede** Vd. cambiarme este dinero?	*Can you change this money for me?*
¿**Puede** Vd. ayudarnos?	*Can you help us?*

Notice that the object pronoun may also be placed before the main verb, **poder**:

| ¿**Nos** pueden dar otra mesa, por favor? | *Can you give us another table, please?* |
| ¿**Me** puede Vd. cambiar este dinero? | *Can you change this money for me?* |

Requests made with **poder** are slightly more formal and polite than those made with the present tense.

Offers

Poder may also be used in making offers, as in:

¿**Puedo** llevarla a su hotel?	*May I take you to your hotel?*
¿**Puedo** hacer algo por Vd.?	*Can I do something for you?*
¿**Podemos** ayudarle?	*Can we help you?*

3 *Querer* used in requests and offers

Requests

Querer (*to want*) is used in requests in sentences like these:

¿Quiere dejarlo/ponerlo aquí, por favor?	*Would you leave/put it here, please?*
¿Quiere esperar/volver a llamar, por favor?	*Would you wait/call again, please?*

Offers

¿Quieres/quiere Vd. una copa?	*Would you like a drink?*
¿Quiere Vd. que le ayude/llame?	*Do you want me to help/call you?*

The last sentence contains a main clause, **¿quiere Vd.?**, and a subordinate clause, **que le ayude/llame. Ayude** (from **ayudar,** *to help*) and **llame** (from **llamar,** *to call*) are in the present subjunctive tense. For an explanation of the subjunctive see Unit 21.

4 *Podría* used in requests

¿**Podría/n...?,** *Could you...?* (singular/plural), a form of the conditional tense (see Unit 22), is often used in making more polite and formal requests:

¿**Podría/n** venir un momento?	*Would you come a moment?* (pol.)
¿**Podría/n** pasar, por favor?	*Would you come in, please?* (pol.)
¿**Podrías** hablar más despacio?	*Could you speak more slowly?*

In context

1 At the hotel reception.

Viajera	Buenas noches. Me marcho mañana a las 8.00. ¿Puede Vd. llamarme a las 7.00, por favor?
Recepcionista	Sí, por supuesto. ¿Le envío el desayuno a la habitación?
Viajera	Sí, por favor. Y me da la factura también. Quiero pagarla ahora mismo.
Recepcionista	De acuerdo, señora.

Viajera	Ah, necesito un taxi para mañana. ¿Puede Vd. llamarme uno para las 8.00 si es tan amable?
Recepcionista	Por supuesto. Es para ir al aeropuerto, ¿verdad?
Viajera	Sí, tengo que estar allí a las 8.45.
Recepcionista	Muy bien, señora. Yo mismo le llamaré uno. No se preocupe Vd.
Viajera	Muchas gracias.

¿le envío el desayuno ...?	*shall I send your breakfast ...?*
si es tan amable	*if you are kind enough*
yo mismo	*I myself*
no se preocupe	*don't worry*

2 A request note.

```
Raúl

¿Puedes pasar por mi despacho antes de irte
a casa? Necesito hablar urgentemente
contigo. Es importante.

Alfonso
```

pasar por	*to drop in*
urgentemente	*urgently*

Practice

1 You are in a hotel in a Spanish-speaking country. Can you make the following requests slightly more informal? Follow the example:

Ejemplo ¿Podría darme la llave de mi habitación?
Por favor, ¿me da la llave de mi habitación?

a ¿Podría traernos dos cafés?
b ¿Podría pasarme el azúcar?
c ¿Podría despertarnos a las 7.00?
d ¿Podría enviarnos el desayuno a la habitación?
e ¿Podría darnos la cuenta?
f ¿Podría llamarme un taxi?

2 Marta Díaz is visiting your company and you are looking after her. How would you make the following offers to her? Use the formal form.

a Shall I help you?
b Shall I bring you a cup of coffee?
c Shall I take you to your hotel?
d Shall I call you tomorrow at 9.00?
e Shall I show you the city?
f Shall I introduce you to the manager?

3 Which of the following phrases would be suitable as a caption for the picture below?

a Tráeme un café.
b ¿Le traigo un café?
c Traiga un café.
d ¿Podría traerme un café?
e ¿Puedo traerle un café?

referring to the recent past

In this unit you will learn how to
- refer to past events which relate to the present
- refer to events which have taken place over a period of time, including the present
- refer to the recent past

Language points
- perfect tense
- *acabar de* + infinitive
- Latin American usage

Key sentences

Referring to past events which relate to the present

Ha recibido/tenido una buena noticia	*He/she has received/had some good news*
¿Quién ha llamado/llegado?	*Who's called/arrived?*

Referring to events which have taken place over a period of time which includes the present

Han estado/trabajado aquí todo el día	*They've been/worked here all day*
Lo he visto/hecho varias veces	*I've seen/done it several times*

Referring to the recent past

He visto/llamado a Nicolás hace un momento	*I saw/called Nicolás a moment ago*
Se han marchado/ido hoy	*They left today*

Grammar summary

1 Perfect tense

Usage

Past events related to the present, for example *She's happy because she's had some good news*, and events which have taken place over a period of time, including the present, as in *They've been here all day*, are normally expressed in English through the perfect tense. Spanish also uses the perfect tense to express the same ideas. Usage differs, however, when referring to the recent past, as in *I saw Peter a while ago*, where Peninsular Spanish favours the use of the perfect tense instead of the simple past.

Formation

To form the perfect tense we use the present tense of **haber** (*to have*) followed by a past participle which is invariable. Remember that the past participle of **-ar** verbs ends in **-ado** while -er and -ir verbs form the past participle by adding -ido to the stem. (For irregular past participles see page 78.) Here are some examples:

estudiar (*to study*)	
he estudiado	*I have studied*
has estudiado	*you have studied* (fam.)
ha estudiado	*you have studied*
	he/she has studied
hemos estudiado	*we have studied*
habéis estudiado	*you have studied* (fam.)
han estudiado	*you/they have studied*

comer (*to eat*)	
he comido	*I have eaten*
has comido	*you have eaten* (fam.)
ha comido	*you have eaten*
	he/she/it has eaten
hemos comido	*we have eaten*
habéis comido	*you have eaten* (fam.)
han comido	*you/they have eaten*

The following examples include regular and irregular forms:

He estudiado/vivido en España	*I have studied/lived in Spain*
Ha comido/bebido demasiado	*He/she has eaten/drunk too much*
Han salido/regresado hace unos minutos	*They went out/came back a few minutes ago*
¿Qué ha dicho/hecho Pedro?	*What did Pedro say/do?*

2 *Acabar de* + infinitive

To express what you have just done, use the verb **acabar** (literally, *to finish*) in the present tense followed by the preposition **de** and an infinitive:

Ella **acaba de** salir	*She has just gone out*
Acabo de llegar	*I've just arrived*
Acabamos de verlo	*We've just seen him*
Acaban de marcharse	*They've just left*

3 Latin American usage

The perfect tense is used much less frequently in Latin America than in Peninsular Spanish. To refer to recent events and to events which are linked to the present, Latin Americans prefer to use the simple past (see Unit 18), for example **terminé** (*I finished*) for **he terminado** (*I have finished*), **¿Viste esta película?** (*Did you see this film?*) for **¿Has visto esta película?** (*Have you seen this film?*). When reference is to events which have occurred over a period of time, including the present, for example **Todavía/aún no hemos terminado** (*We still haven't finished*), the tendency is to use the perfect tense. Bear in mind, however, that there are regional variations.

In context

1 Isabel is looking for her friend Enrique.

Isabel Buenas tardes. ¿Está Enrique?

Señora Lo siento, pero Enrique no está. Acaba de salir. Ha ido a casa de José.

Isabel Por favor, ¿puede Vd. decirle que lo he venido a buscar para ir a la piscina? Lo esperaré allí.

Señora Bueno, se lo diré.

> **lo he venido a buscar** *I've come for him*

2 What have you done today?

Él ¿Qué has hecho hoy?

Ella Esta mañana he estado en la biblioteca un rato y he terminado de escribir un artículo para la clase de mañana. Luego he ido a la peluquería. Acabo de regresar. ¿Y tú qué has hecho?

Él Hoy me he levantado muy tarde y me he quedado en casa leyendo. ¿Has comido ya?

Ella No, todavía no. No he tenido tiempo de preparar nada.

Él Entonces, ¿qué te parece si vamos a comer algo? Podemos ir al bar de Pepe.

Ella De acuerdo, vamos.

Notice the position of the pronouns in the following sentences. Pronouns always precede the construction with the perfect tense.

Me he levantado tarde.   *I got up late.*
Me he quedado en casa.   *I stayed at home.*

Practice

1 Can you make sense of these sentences? Match the phrases on the left with an appropriate phrase from the right, and then give the infinitive corresponding to each verb.

a Le he escrito...   1 ...sus nuevas gafas.
b Antonio nos ha dicho...   2 ...las tiendas.
c Carmen ha roto...   3 ...una carta a Manuel.
d José ha vuelto...   4 ...el dinero en el banco.
e Todavía no han hecho...   5 ...la verdad.
f Han abierto...   6 ...de sus vacaciones.
g He puesto...   7 ...sus reservas.

2 You phone your friend Ana to make arrangements to go to the cinema. Use the following guidelines to fill in your part of the conversation with her.

Voz ¿Dígame?
Tú *Say hello and who you are, and ask whether Ana is in.*
Voz Sí, acaba de llegar. Un momento, por favor.
Ana Hola, ¿qué tal?
Tú *Say hello to Ana and ask her whether she's free tonight.*
Ana Sí, ¿por qué?
Tú *Ask her whether she's seen the new Almodóvar film. You've been told it's very good.*
Ana No, todavía no la he visto, pero quisiera verla.
Tú *Say you've phoned the cinema and they've told you that there's a show (**una sesión**) at 9.00. Ask her what she thinks.*
Ana Sí, a las 9.00 me parece bien.

3 While on holiday, Sarah writes a letter to a Spanish-speaking friend. Fill in the blank spaces in the letter with a suitable verb from those accompanying the pictures. The first two have been done for you.

Hola Carlos:

¿Qué tal estás? Te escribo para contarte que Tom y yo <u>hemos venido</u> de vacaciones a España y hasta ahora lo <u>hemos pasado</u> estupendamente bien. .... a la playa casi todos los días y el fin de semana pasado .... un coche/carro (L. Am.) para salir de paseo. Hoy por la mañana, (yo) .... un rato en el mar y después Tom y yo .... a caballo. Por la tarde .... vela.

a venir, pasar

b ir

c alquilar

d nadar

e montar

f hacer

referring to past events

In this unit you will learn how to
- refer to events which are past and complete
- refer to events which lasted over a definite period of time and ended in the past

Language points
- preterite tense
- adverbs of time associated with the preterite
- *hace* in time phrases
- historic present

Key sentences

Actions which happened and were completed in the past, as in *They went to Cuba last year*, and events which lasted over a definite period of time and ended in the past, for example *She lived in Spain for seven years*, are expressed in Spanish through the preterite tense or simple past.

Referring to events which are past and complete

¿Cuándo saliste/llegaste?	*When did you leave/arrive?*
Salí/llegué hace una hora	*I left/arrived an hour ago*
El año pasado viajaron/ fueron a Cuba	*Last year they travelled/ went to Cuba*

Referring to events which lasted over a definite period of time and ended in the past

Vivió/estuvo siete años en España	*He/she lived/was in Spain for seven years*
Trabajamos/estudiamos juntos durante dos años	*We worked/studied together for two years*

Grammar summary

1 Preterite tense

Formation

There are two sets of endings for this tense, one for **-ar** verbs and another one for verbs in **-er** and **-ir**.

viajar (*to travel*)	
viajé	*I travelled*
viajaste	*you travelled* (fam.)
viajó	*you/he/she travelled*
viajamos	*we travelled*
viajasteis	*you travelled* (fam.)
viajaron	*you/they travelled*

Note that the 1st person plural, **viajamos,** is the same as for the present tense.

responder (to answer)	
respondí	I answered
respondiste	you answered (fam.)
respondió	you/he/she answered
respondimos	we answered
respondisteis	you answered (fam.)
respondieron	you/they answered

recibir (to receive)	
recibí	I received
recibiste	you received (fam.)
recibió	you/he/she received
recibimos	we received
recibisteis	you received (fam.)
recibieron	you/they received

Note that the 1st person plural, **recibimos,** is the same as for the present tense.

El año pasado **viajé** a Perú	Last year I travelled to Peru
Él **viajó** por más de una semana	He travelled for more than a week
Ayer **respondí** a la carta de Esteban	I answered Esteban's letter yesterday
Carlos no **respondió** a mi carta	Carlos didn't answer my letter
¿Cuándo **recibiste** el paquete?	When did you receive the parcel?
Lo **recibí** el martes pasado	I received it last Tuesday

Irregular preterite forms

Some verbs have an irregular preterite. Here is a list of the most important:

andar (to walk)	anduve, anduviste, anduvo, anduvimos, anduvisteis, anduvieron
dar (to give)	di, diste, dio, dimos, disteis, dieron
decir (to say)	dije, dijiste, dijo, dijimos, dijisteis, dijeron
estar (to be)	estuve, estuviste, estuvo, estuvimos, estuvisteis, estuvieron

haber (*to have*, aux.)	hube, hubiste, hubo,
	hubimos, hubisteis, hubieron
hacer (*to do, make*)	hice, hiciste, hizo,
	hicimos, hicisteis, hicieron
ir (*to go*)	fui, fuiste, fue,
	fuimos, fuisteis, fueron
obtener (*to get*)	obtuve, obtuviste, obtuvo,
	obtuvimos, obtuvisteis, obtuvieron
poder (*to be able*)	pude, pudiste, pudo,
	pudimos, pudisteis, pudieron
poner (*to put*)	puse, pusiste, puso,
	pusimos, pusisteis, pusieron
querer (*to want*)	quise, quisiste, quiso,
	quisimos, quisisteis, quisieron
saber (*to know*)	supe, supiste, supo,
	supimos, supisteis, supieron
ser (*to be*)	fui, fuiste, fue,
	fuimos, fuisteis, fueron
tener (*to have*)	tuve, tuviste, tuvo,
	tuvimos, tuvisteis, tuvieron
traer (*to bring*)	traje, trajiste, trajo,
	trajimos, trajisteis, trajeron
venir (*to come*)	vine, viniste, vino,
	vinimos, vinisteis, vinieron

For a list of the most common irregular verbs see pages
203–6.

¿Qué **hiciste** ayer?	*What did you do yesterday?*
Fui a casa de Manolo	*I went to Manolo's house*
¿Dónde **estuvisteis** este verano?	*Where were you this summer?*
Estuvimos en San Francisco	*We were in San Francisco*
¿Qué le **diste** a Roberto para su cumpleaños?	*What did you give Roberto for his birthday?*
Le **di** una corbata	*I gave him a tie*

Spelling changes in the preterite tense

Some verbs need a change in the spelling in the 1st person
singular to enable the final consonant of the stem to keep the
same sound as in the infinitive. Some of these verbs are:

| llegar | *to arrive* | llegué | *I arrived* |
| pagar | *to pay* | pagué | *I paid* |

| sacar | *to get, e.g. tickets* | saqué | *I got* |
| tocar | *to play an instrument* | toqué | *I played* |

A spelling change may also occur because of an accent in the infinitive or because there would otherwise be more than two vowels together:

caer (*to fall*)	caí, caíste, cayó,
	caímos, caísteis, cayeron
leer (*to read*)	leí, leíste, leyó,
	leímos, leísteis, leyeron
oír (*to hear*)	oí, oíste, oyó,
	oímos, oísteis, oyeron

Llegué hace dos semanas	*I arrived two weeks ago*
Pagué la cuenta anoche	*I paid the bill last night*
Saqué dos entradas para el cine	*I got two tickets for the cinema*
Ella no **leyó** la carta	*She didn't read the letter*

2 Adverbs of time and time phrases normally associated with the preterite tense

The following adverbs of time and time phrases often occur in sentences with a verb in the preterite tense:

ayer	*yesterday*
anteayer	*the day before yesterday*
anoche	*last night*
el lunes/martes pasado	*last Monday/Tuesday*
la semana pasada	*last week*
el mes/el año pasado	*last month/year*
en 1975/en 1999	*in 1975/in 1999*
hace dos meses/tres años	*two months/three years ago*

Some of these time phrases may also occur with other tenses, for example the imperfect tense (see Unit 19).

3 *Hace* in time phrases

With a verb in the preterite tense, **hace** translates into English as *ago*:

Vivió aquí **hace** dos años   *He/she lived here two years ago*

| **Hace** seis meses que llegó | *He/she arrived six months ago* |
| ¿Cuánto tiempo **hace** que pasó? | *How long ago did it happen?* |

Compare this construction with the one you learned in Unit 8, in which **hace** is used with a verb in the present tense:

| Vive aquí desde **hace** dos años | *He/she has been living here for two years* |

4 Historic present

The present tense is frequently used in narrative contexts (e.g. literature, history) with a past meaning in order to lend more force to the actions or events being described. It is also present in colloquial language.

Written language

En noviembre de 1975 muere el general Francisco Franco y el príncipe Juan Carlos pasa a ocupar el trono de España. El país empieza a vivir una serie de cambios de orden político y social...

General Francisco Franco died in November 1975 and Prince Juan Carlos occupied the Spanish throne. The country began to undergo a series of political and social changes...

Spoken language

Esta mañana en el metro he visto a Antonia. ¿Sabes qué?, se acerca a mí y me dice que siente mucho lo ocurrido ...

This morning, in the underground, I saw Antonia. You know, she came up to me and told me that she was very sorry about what happened...

In both of these examples, depending on the context, the present tense could be used in the English translation.

In context

1 What did you do on your holiday?

Marisol	¿Qué hiciste en tus vacaciones?
Fernando	Estuve unos días en Inglaterra en casa de unos amigos.
Marisol	¿Fuiste solo?
Fernando	No, fui con Ángela.

Marisol	¿Y qué os pareció Londres?
Fernando	Nos gustó muchísimo. Lo pasamos estupenda-mente. Y tú, ¿has estado alguna vez en Inglaterra?
Marisol	Sí, estuve allí hace cuatro años. Hice un curso de inglés en Brighton y viví un mes con una familia inglesa. Lo pasé muy bien. Pienso volver el año que viene.

¿qué os pareció Londres?	*what did you think of London?*
lo pasamos estupendamente	*we had a very good time*
alguna vez	*ever*
lo pasé muy bien	*I had a good time*

2 The manager has been away from the office for a few days. On his return he talks to his secretary.

Gerente	¿Hay algún recado para mí?
Secretaria	Sí, el lunes llamó el señor Solís para pedir una cita con usted. Vendrá mañana a las 10.00. También hubo una llamada del señor Francisco Riquelme de México. Dice que llegará a Madrid el viernes a las 2.00 de la tarde.
Gerente	¿Han traído el nuevo ordenador?
Secretaria	Sí, lo trajeron ayer. Lo dejaron en su despacho. Aquí está la factura.

¿hay algún recado?	*is there any message?*
pedir una cita	*to ask for an appointment*
hubo una llamada	*there was a call*

Observe the contrast between the perfect tense and the preterite tense in these two sentences:

Y tú, ¿has estado alguna vez   *And have you ever been to*
en Inglaterra?   *England?*
Estuve allí hace cuatro años   *I was there four years ago*

The two tenses are not interchangeable in these sentences. Words such as **alguna vez** (*ever*), **nunca** (*never*) require the use of the perfect tense because they somehow establish a relationship with the present: **alguna vez** (*ever*) is equivalent in meaning to **hasta ahora** (*so far*). In the second sentence, the preterite tense is obligatory because it refers to an event which is past and complete.

Practice

1 In a letter to a friend, Silvia writes about her holidays. Fill in the blanks with a suitable verb from the list using the preterite tense.

ser	estar
invitar	volver
pasar	parecer
ir	gustar
traer	conocer

Querido Ignacio

Hace sólo una semana (1) (yo) ... de México, y no sabes lo bien que lo (2) ... . (3) ... en casa de unos parientes de mi madre que viven en Guadalajara. Me (4) ... mucho la ciudad. Y la gente me (5) ... muy amable. En mi última semana allí (6) ... con mis parientes a Puerto Vallarta. ¡Es una ciudad preciosa! Allí (7) (nosotros) ... a unos mexicanos que me (8) ... a pasar unos días en su casa en Guanajuato. Creo que éstas (9) ... las mejores vacaciones de mi vida (10) (yo) ... muchas fotos de México. Te las enseñaré ...

2 Your Spanish boss is checking on your progress. Answer his/her questions using the preterite tense and the time phrases in brackets. Follow the example.

Ejemplo ¿Ha enviado Vd. las cartas? (ayer)
　　　　　Sí, las envié ayer

a ¿Ha escrito Vd. el informe? (anteayer)
b ¿Ha hecho Vd. las reservas de hotel? (el lunes)
c ¿Ha llamado Vd. a la señora Miranda? (ayer por la mañana)
d ¿Ha comprado Vd. el material de oficina? (la semana pasada)
e ¿Ha mandado Vd. el fax a Buenos Aires? (anoche)
f ¿Ha respondido Vd. la carta del señor Lira? (anteanoche/ antenoche L.Am.)

3 Here are some of the things Carmen and Pablo did in the office yesterday. Look at the pictures and write an appropriate sentence for each picture, saying what each one did. Choose from the phrases below and follow the example.

---

enviar faxes   servir café a los clientes   contestar el teléfono
trabajar en el ordenador/la computadora (L. Am.)
leer la correspondencia   atender al público

Ejemplo (llamar por teléfono a un cliente)
Carmen llamó por teléfono a un cliente.

16

describing the past

In this unit you will learn how to

- describe things, places and people known in the past
- describe actions which were taking place when something else happened
- describe states or actions which were habitual in the past
- describe states or actions which occurred before some past event

Language points

- imperfect tense
- imperfect continuous
- pluperfect tense
- *soler* + infinitive for past reference
- *acostumbrar* + infinitive for past reference

Key sentences

This unit introduces two new tenses, the imperfect tense and the pluperfect, both used with reference to the past. The imperfect, as found in sentences such as **Era bonito**, *It was pretty*, **Estaba trabajando cuando...**, *I was working when...*, **Nos visitaban siempre**, *They always used to visit us*, has no direct correspondence in English. The pluperfect, as in **Ya habíamos salido**, *We had already gone out*, is used in much the same way as the English pluperfect.

Describing things, places and people known in the past

Era/eran caro/s	*It was/they were expensive*
Tenía/había dos habitaciones	*It had/there were two rooms*

Describing actions which were taking place when something else happened

¿Qué estabas haciendo/ hacías cuando ocurrió?	*What were you doing when it happened?*
Estaba leyendo/leía cuando él llamó	*I was/he/she was reading when he called*

Describing states or actions which were habitual in the past

Venían/viajaban a Mallorca todos los años	*They used to come/travel to Mallorca every year*
Nos levantábamos/ marchábamos a las 7.00 todos los días	*We used to get up/leave at 7.00 every day*

Describing states or actions which occurred before some past event

La reunión había empezado/ terminado cuando llegué	*The meeting had begun/ finished when I arrived*
¿Habías estado/venido aquí antes?	*Had you been/come here before?*

Grammar summary

1 Imperfect tense

Uses

In general terms, the imperfect tense is used for actions which were taking place in the past and whose beginning or end are not specified. Unlike the preterite, which commonly indicates completed past events, the imperfect denotes actions which were incomplete. Consider these two sentences:

En aquel tiempo yo trabajaba en Barcelona	*At that time I used to work in Barcelona*
Entre enero y junio de ese año trabajé en Barcelona	*Between January and June of that year I worked in Barcelona*

In the first example, the beginning and end of the action are not specified. In the second we are referring to a completed past event.

More specifically, the imperfect tense is used to describe things, places and people with reference to the past, to describe actions which were taking place when something else happened (the second action will normally be expressed in the preterite) and to describe states or actions which were habitual in the past.

Formation

There are two sets of endings for the imperfect tense, one for -**ar** verbs and another one for verbs endings in -**er** and -**ir**.

trabajar *(to work)*	
trabajaba	*I worked/used to work*
trabajabas	*you worked/used to work* (fam.)
trabajaba	*you/he/she worked/used to work*
trabajábamos	*we worked/used to work*
trabajabais	*you worked/used to work* (fam.)
trabajaban	*you/they worked/used to work*

Note that the 1st and 3rd person singular share the same endings.

tener *(to have)*	
tenía	*I had/used to have*
tenías	*you had/used to have* (fam.)
tenía	*you/he/she/it had/used to have*
teníamos	*we had/used to have*
teníais	*you had/used to have* (fam.)
tenían	*you/they had/used to have*

vivir *(to live)*	
vivía	*I lived/used to live*
vivías	*you lived/used to live* (fam.)
vivía	*you/he/she lived/used to live*
vivíamos	*we lived/used to live*
vivíais	*you lived/used to live* (fam.)
vivían	*you/they lived/used to live*

Note that the 1st and 3rd person singular share the same endings.

¿Dónde **trabajabas** antes?	*Where did you work/were you working before?*
Trabajaba en una fábrica	*I worked/was working/used to work in a factory*
¿Qué coche **tenía** Vd. antes? **Tenía** un Seat	*What car did you have before? I had a Seat*
¿Dónde **vivíais** antes de llegar aquí?	*Where did you live before arriving here?*
Vivíamos en Toledo	*We lived/used to live in Toledo*

Irregular imperfect forms

There are only three irregular verbs in the imperfect tense, **ir** *(to go)*, **ser** *(to be)* and **ver** *(to see)*:

ir	ser	ver
iba	era	veía
ibas (fam.)	eras (fam.)	veías (fam.)
iba	era	veía
íbamos	éramos	veíamos
ibais (fam.)	erais (fam.)	veíais
iban	eran	veían

For a list of the most common irregular verbs in all tenses see pages 203–6.

Yo **iba** al colegio cuando ocurrió el accidente	*I was going to school when the accident happened*
¿Cómo **era** la casa?	*What was the house like?*
Era una casa grande y moderna y **tenía** un gran jardín	*It was a big modern house and it had a large garden*
Francisca y yo nos **veíamos** casi todos los días	*Francisca and I used to see each other almost every day*

2 Imperfect continuous

Usage

To make it clear we are referring to an action which was in progress when something else happened, for example *I was eating when he called me*, we can use the imperfect continuous as an alternative to the imperfect tense.

Formation

The imperfect continuous is formed with the imperfect form of **estar** followed by a gerund (for the gerund, see Unit 8). Here are some examples:

Ella **estaba preparando** el almuerzo cuando él entró	*She was preparing lunch when he came in*
Nosotros **estábamos durmiendo** cuando ocurrió el robo	*We were sleeping when the theft took place*
¿Qué **estabas haciendo** allí?	*What were you doing there?*
Estaba hablando con Marta	*I was talking to Marta*

3 Pluperfect tense

Usage

The Spanish pluperfect tense is equivalent to the English pluperfect and it is normally used to describe states or actions which occurred before some past event, as in *Her mother had died when John was born*.

Formation

The pluperfect tense is formed with the imperfect form of **haber** (**había, habías, había, habíamos, habíais, habían**) followed by a past participle which is invariable (for the formation of past participles, see Unit 11).

La fiesta ya **había empezado** cuando nosotros entramos	*The party had already started when we went in*
No aceptamos su invitación pues ya **habíamos visto** la película	*We didn't accept their invitation because we had already seen the film*
La carrera ya **había terminado** cuando empezó a llover	*The race had already finished when it started to rain*

4 *Soler* + infinitive and *acostumbrar (a)* + infinitive for past reference

Soler and **acostumbrar** (see Unit 9) may be used in the imperfect tense to refer to an action which was habitual in the past:

¿Qué **solías** hacer?	*What did you usually do?*
Solía leer mucho	*I used to read a lot*
Solíamos vernos regularmente	*We used to see each other regularly*
Acostumbraban (a) venir una vez por semana	*They used to come once a week*
Acostumbrábamos (a) dar largos paseos	*We used to go for long walks*

In context

1 Remembering the past.

Ignacio ¿Cuánto tiempo hace que vives aquí?

Eliana Hace dos años solamente.

Ignacio ¿Y dónde vivías antes?

Eliana Vivía en Nueva York.

Ignacio ¡En Nueva York! ¿Y qué hacías allí?

Eliana Trabajaba en un colegio como profesora de español, y al mismo tiempo estudiaba inglés en la universidad. Con lo que ganaba como profesora pagaba mis estudios y el alquiler de un apartamento.

Ignacio ¿Vivías sola?

Eliana No, compartía el apartamento con dos colegas. Uno era español y el otro colombiano.

Ignacio ¿Hablabas ya inglés cuando llegaste allí?

Eliana Lo hablaba bastante mal y entendía muy poco, pero conseguí aprender bastante.

al mismo tiempo	at the same time
con lo que ganaba	with what I earned
un/una colega	colleague
conseguí aprender	I managed to learn

2 Read this extract from a short story.

Eran ya las 9.00 de la noche cuando Lucía llegó a la casa de la señora Velarde. Hacía frío y la lluvia empezaba a caer. Lucía llamó a la puerta tres veces pero nadie respondió. La señora Rosario Velarde era una mujer mayor, tenía unos ochenta años, y vivía sola con su perro Damián. Lucía llamó otra vez, pero nadie respondió. Dentro de la casa había luz y por la ventana se veía el pequeño salón ...

la lluvia empezaba a caer	the rain was starting to fall
llamó a la puerta	she knocked at the door
una mujer mayor	an old woman
tenía unos ochenta años	she was about eighty years old
había luz	there was a light
por la ventana	through the window
el salón	sitting room

Notice the use of the imperfect and preterite tenses in the second text:

hacía frío	*it was cold*
la lluvia empezaba a caer	*the rain was starting to fall*
Lucía llamó a la puerta	*Lucia knocked at the door*
nadie respondió	*no one answered*

Here, the imperfect tense is descriptive while the preterite serves to indicate a series of completed past events.

Practice

1 Tomás tells a friend about someone special he knew long ago. Complete his description with the right form of the verb in brackets.

(1) (Llamarse) Elena, (2) (tener) 28 años, (3) (ser) alta, delgada y muy guapa y (4) (vestir) muy bien. Elena (5) (ser) enfermera y cuando la conocí (6) (trabajar) en un hospital cerca de casa. Elena (7) (compartir) un apartamento con una

amiga. El apartamento (8) (ser) pequeño, pero (9) (tener) una vista maravillosa. En aquel tiempo Elena (10) (estudiar) piano y (11) (tocar) muy bien. A mí me (12) (gustar) mucho oírla tocar.

Now use this passage as a model to describe someone you knew.

2 Victoria used to live and work in England. Read this account of her life there and choose the correct tense.

(1) (Llegué/llegaba) a Londres en el año 1986. En aquel tiempo (2) (tuve/tenía) 22 años e/y* (3) (hizo/hacía) sólo seis meses que (4) (terminaba/había terminado) mis estudios de Derecho. Al llegar a Inglaterra (5) (supe/sabía) muy poco inglés y lo primero que (6) (hice/hacía) al llegar a Londres (7) (fue/era) tomar clases de inglés.

El primer mes (8) (me quedé/me quedaba) en casa de unos amigos españoles, hasta que (9) (encontré/encontraba) una habitación donde vivir. Pero Londres (10) (fue/era) una ciudad muy cara y yo no (11) (tuve/tenía) mucho dinero. Un amigo me (12) (ayudó/ayudaba) a encontrar un trabajo donde (13) (gané/ganaba) lo suficiente para vivir. Allí (14) (trabajé/trabajaba) durante seis meses ...

Try writing a brief passage about a period in your own life.

*y changes to e before i or hi (except for hie-).

3 This is the house where Ana and her family used to live. Fill in the blanks in the description with an appropriate verb from the box.

haber	gustar	tener	ser	estar

La casa de Ana era muy bonita, ... en medio del campo y .... dos plantas. No .... una casa muy grande, pero .... muy cómoda. Delante de la casa .... un jardín y detrás de ella .... una colina. Sobre la colina .... unos árboles. Los padres de Ana .... un coche y Ana .... una bicicleta. Ana .... un perro. Al perro le .... jugar en el jardín.

20

giving directions and instructions

In this unit you will learn
how to
- ask and give directions
- give commands and
  instructions

Language points
- imperative
- present tense used in
  directions
- infinitive used in directions

Key sentences

We can give directions and instructions in a variety of ways in English, for example: *You have to/can turn left, Go straight on, Wait for the dialling tone.* Spanish also has a number of ways of giving directions and instructions. These involve some of the constructions you learned in previous units.

Asking for directions

¿Dónde está el banco/correos?	*Where's the bank/post office?*
¿Puede decirme dónde está el museo/la catedral?	*Can you tell me where the museum/cathedral is?*
¿Sabe Vd./sabes dónde está?	*Do you know where it is?*
¿Por dónde se va al aeropuerto/a la estación?	*Can you tell me the way to the airport/station?* (Literally, *Which way does one go …?*)

Giving directions

Está en la esquina/al final de esta calle	*It's on the corner/at the end of this road*
Tiene que/puede girar a la izquierda/derecha	*You have to/can turn left/right*
Siga todo recto/hasta el semáforo	*Go straight on/as far as the traffic lights*
Coja (*Spain*)/tome esta calle	*Take this road*

Giving commands and instructions

Abre/abra (Vd.) la ventana	*Open the window*
No tardes/tarde (Vd.) mucho	*Don't take too long*
Espera/espere (Vd.) el tono de marcar	*Wait for the dialling tone*

Grammar summary

1 Imperative

Uses

The imperative is the form most commonly associated with directions, commands and instructions. Now study the formation of the imperative and consider again the **Key sentences** and the examples following.

Formation: polite imperatives

In Spanish we use different imperative forms depending on who we are talking to (polite or familiar) and whether we are speaking to one or more than one person (singular or plural). To form the imperative we use the stem of the 1st person singular of the present tense plus the appropriate ending. Here are the polite imperatives of three regular verbs, **girar** (*to turn*), **responder** (*to answer*), and **subir** (*to go up*), representing each of the three conjugations:

Present tense (1st person)	Imperative	
giro	gire	*turn* (sing.)
	giren	*turn* (pl.)
respondo	responda	*answer* (sing.)
	respondan	*answer* (pl.)
subo	suba	*go up* (sing.)
	suban	*go up* (pl.)

The negative imperative is formed by placing **no** before the verb: **no** gire (*don't turn*), **no** responda (*don't answer*), **no** suba (*don't go up*).

The following examples contain only regular verbs:

-ar	(girar)	**Gire/n** a la derecha	*Turn left*
	(continuar)	**Continúe/n** por esta calle	*Continue along this street*
	(cambiar)	**Cambie/n** este dinero	*Change this money*
-er	(responder)	**Responda/n** a estas cartas	*Answer these letters*
	(leer)	**Lea/n** las instrucciones	*Read the instructions*
	(correr)	No **corra/n**	*Do not run*
-ir	(subir)	**Suba/n** al segundo piso	*Go up to the second floor*
	(escribir)	**Escriba/n** al señor García	*Write to señor García*
	(abrir)	**Abra/n** la puerta	*Open the door*

Observe that 1st conjugation verbs (**-ar**) acquire the endings of 2nd conjugation verbs (**-er**) while 2nd and 3rd conjugation verbs (**-er** and **-ir**) acquire the endings of the 1st conjugation.

The pronoun **Vd.** or **Vds.** is often added after the verb in order to soften the command:

gire Vd. a la izquierda *turn left*
continúen Vds. por esta calle *continue along this street*

Irregular polite imperatives

As the imperative is formed with the stem of the 1st person singular of the present tense, verbs which are irregular in the present are also irregular in the imperative. This rule also applies to stem-changing verbs. Here are some examples:

Infinitive		Present	Imperative (sing./pl.)
seguir	(*to follow*)	sigo	siga/n
cerrar	(*to close*)	cierro	cierre/n
dar	(*to give*)	doy	dé/den
estar	(*to be*)	estoy	esté/n
hacer	(*to do, make*)	hago	haga/n
poner	(*to put*)	pongo	ponga/n
traer	(*to bring*)	traigo	traiga/n
volver	(*to return*)	vuelvo	vuelva/n
conducir	(*to drive*)	conduzco	conduzca/n
decir	(*to say*)	digo	diga/n
oír	(*to hear*)	oigo	oiga/n
salir	(*to go out*)	salgo	salga/n
seguir	(*to follow*)	sigo	siga/n
venir	(*to come*)	vengo	venga/n

Venga/n mañana   *Come tomorrow*
Conduzca/n con cuidado   *Drive carefully*
No haga/n eso   *Don't do that*
Vuelva/n el martes   *Come back on Tuesday*
Cierre/n la puerta   *Close the door*

Ir, saber and ser

Ir (*to go*), **saber** (*to know*) and **ser** (*to be*) form the imperative in a different way:

Infinitive		Present	Imperative (sing./pl.)
ir	(*to go*)	voy	vaya/n
saber	(*to know*)	sé	sepa/n
ser	(*to be*)	soy	sea/n

Vaya a la recepción	*Go to the reception*
Sépase que no lo haré otra vez	*Let it be known that I won't do it again*
Sean Vds. puntuales, por favor	*Be punctual, please*

Observe the passive **se** attached to the imperative form **sepa**. The addition of a syllable to the word requires the use of an accent in the third syllable from the end (see Pronouns with imperative on page 144).

Spelling changes

Note the following spelling changes in verbs ending in **-car**, **-gar** and **-ger**:

Infinitive		Present	Imperative (sing./pl.)
buscar	(*to look for*)	busco	busque/n
tocar	(*to touch, play*)	toco	toque/n
pagar	(*to pay*)	pago	pague/n
llegar	(*to arrive*)	llego	llegue/n
coger	(*to take, catch*)	cojo	coja/n

Busque la llave	*Look for the key*
Pague Vd. ahora	*Pay now*
Por favor **lleguen** a la hora	*Please arrive on time*

Familiar imperatives

Familiar imperatives have different positive and negative forms. Some examples of positive familiar forms are:

Infinitive		Present	Imperative (sing./pl.)
girar	(*to turn*)	giro	gira/d
responder	(*to answer*)	respondo	responde/d
subir	(*to go up*)	subo	sube/subid

Examples

Gira a la izquierda	*Turn left* (sing.)
Girad a la derecha	*Turn right* (pl.)
Responde pronto	*Answer soon* (sing.)
Responded rápido	*Answer quickly* (pl.)
Sube al primer piso	*Go up to the first floor* (sing.)
Subid por esta calle	*Go up this road* (pl.)

Some examples of negative familiar forms are:

Infinitive		Present	Imperative (sing./pl.)
girar	(*to turn*)	giro	no gires
			no giréis
responder	(*to answer*)	respondo	no respondas
			no respondáis
subir	(*to go up*)	subo	no subas
			no subáis

No **giréis** aquí, **girad** en la esquina	*Do not turn here, turn at the corner* (pl.)
No **respondas** hoy, **responde** mañana	*Do not reply today, reply tomorrow* (sing.)
No **subáis** al primer piso, **subid** al segundo	*Don't go up to the first floor, go up to the second* (pl.)

Irregular familiar imperatives

The following verbs form the singular positive familiar imperative in an irregular way.

decir	(*to say*)	di
hacer	(*to do, make*)	haz
ir	(*to go*)	ve
oír	(*to hear*)	oye
poner	(*to put*)	pon
salir	(*to go out*)	sal
ser	(*to be*)	sé
tener	(*to have*)	ten
venir	(*to come*)	ven

Haz lo que digo	*Do what I say*
Ve inmediatamente	*Go immediately*
¡Oye!	*Listen!*
¡Sal de aquí!	*Get out of here!*
Ven aquí un momento	*Come here a moment*

Plural forms are regular, for example **¡venid!** *come!*

Pronouns with imperative

If the imperative includes a pronoun, this must go at the end of the positive form but before the negative one. Positive imperatives which carry a pronoun may need to add an accent.

Dígale que necesito verla	*Tell her I need to see her*
No lo traiga hoy	*Do not bring it today*
Tráigalo mañana	*Bring it tomorrow*
No lo haga así	*Don't do it like this*
Hágalo de esta manera	*Do it this way*
Llámame a las 6.00	*Call me at 6.00*

2 Present tense used in directions

One simple and frequent way of giving directions is by using the present tense (for its forms see Units 7 and 8) instead of the imperative. Look at these examples:

Vd. coge/toma la segunda calle a la izquierda	*You take the second turning on the left*
Vd. sube/baja hasta la tercera planta	*You go up/down to the third floor*

3 Infinitive used in directions

Directions and instructions are sometimes given through the use of infinitives. This is particularly common in the written language, for example in notices, advertisements and traffic signals.

No fumar	*Do not smoke*
No adelantar/aparcar	*Do not overtake/park*
Tomar un comprimido con cada comida	*Take one tablet with each meal*

In context

1 Asking the way.

Turista   ¿La oficina de turismo, por favor?

Policía   Siga Vd. todo recto por esta calle hasta el final, allí gire Vd. a la izquierda y continúe por esa misma calle hasta el segundo semáforo. La oficina de turismo está en la esquina.

por esta calle	*along this street*
esa misma calle	*that same street*

2 Giving instructions in the office.

Jefe	Teresa, venga a mi despacho un momento, por favor.
Secretaria	Sí, ¿dígame?
Jefe	Mire, vaya al banco e ingrese estos cheques en mi cuenta corriente y después vaya a correos y eche estas cartas. Antes de volver pase por la papelería y tráigame el material de oficina que pedimos ayer. Ah, y pregunte en la agencia de viajes si está lista mi reserva para Buenos Aires...

mire	*look*
ingrese (ingresar)	*deposit (to deposit)*
pase por (pasar)	*stop by (to stop by)*
pedimos (pedir)	*we ordered (to order)*
si está listo/a	*if it's ready*

Because of their formal context, the polite imperative form has been used in both dialogues:

siga Vd. todo recto	*go straight on*
gire Vd. a la izquierda	*turn left*
vaya al banco	*go to the bank*
eche estas cartas	*post these letters*

Practice

1 In a familiar context, you need to use the informal imperative. Practise changing the formal imperatives in dialogues 1 and 2 in this unit into the familiar form, as if talking to a friend.

2 A Spanish-speaking friend is moving house and you are helping him/her. Complete your friend's instructions by changing the infinitives in brackets into the familiar imperative form. Follow the example:

Ejemplo No (abrir) esta habitación ahora. (Abrir) la después.
          No abras esta habitación ahora. Ábrela después.

a No (poner) esa caja en el comedor. (Poner) la en el salón.
b No (dejar) esas cosas aquí. (Llevar) las a la cocina.

c No (traer) las maletas al salón. (Dejar) las en el dormitorio.

d No (cerrar) esa ventana. (Cerrar) la otra.

e No (limpiar) la cocina todavía. (Hacer) lo después.

f No (ir) al supermercado ahora. (Ir) más tarde.

g No (hacer) la limpieza todavía. (Hacer) la en otro momento.

h No (tirar) esa caja todavía. (Esperar) un momento.

3 A Spanish-speaking friend who is visiting your home town needs to get to the station. Follow the arrows in the picture and tell your friend how to get there.

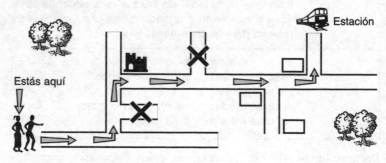

21

expressing emotional reactions, possibility and doubt

In this unit you will learn how to
- express emotional reactions: hope, fear, regret, satisfaction
- express possibility
- express doubt or uncertainty
- express emotional reactions, possibility and doubt with reference to the recent past

Language points
- subjunctive
- present subjunctive
- verbs and phrases denoting emotion
- subjunctive or indicative
- perfect subjunctive

Key sentences

In English, emotional reactions such as hope, regret, satisfaction, may be expressed through sentences such as *She hopes he answers soon, I'm sorry they can't come, I'm glad she's here*. These sentences contain two clauses: a main clause with a verb in the present tense (e.g. *she hopes...*), followed by another clause with a verb which is also in the present tense (e.g. *... (that) he answers soon*).

Sentences which express possibility and doubt have a similar structure, for example: *It's possible that they may get married, I doubt that he has the money*.

Spanish differs somewhat from English in the way it expresses these ideas. In the main clause there is no variation. As in English, the main verb may be in the present, the past or the future, but the linking word **que** (*that*, in English), which introduces the second clause, known as the *subordinate clause*, may not be omitted. If the subject of the subordinate clause is different from that of the main clause (e.g. *she hopes that he answers*) then the verb in the subordinate clause must be in the subjunctive. This is an alternative form of the verb, not a tense.

The subjunctive covers a range of tenses – present, imperfect, perfect and pluperfect subjunctive – which are different from the tenses you have learned so far in this book, and which grammar books refer to as tenses of the *indicative*.

Expressing emotional reactions

Ella espera que él responda/ escriba pronto	*She hopes he answers/ writes soon*
Siento que no vengan/viajen	*I'm sorry they can't come/ travel*
Me alegro de que ella esté/ trabaje aquí	*I'm glad she is/works here*

Expressing possibility

Es posible que se casen/ divorcien	*It's possible that they may get married/divorced*
Es probable que lluova/nieve	*It'll probably rain/snow*

Expressing doubt or uncertainty

No creo que lo compren/ vendan	*I don't think they'll buy/sell it*
Dudo que él tenga/consiga el dinero	*I doubt that he has/he'll get the money*

Grammar summary

1 The subjunctive

General usage

The subjunctive is generally associated with a subordinate clause introduced by **que** which is dependent on a main clause. The main clause usually carries the type of verb which calls for the use of the subjunctive in the subordinate clause, for example, verbs expressing emotion, possibility and doubt (see earlier examples).

The subjunctive may also occur in clauses introduced by **que**, for example when the antecedent is not known, as in:

Buscamos una secretaria **que hable** inglés	*We're looking for s secretary who speaks English*
Queremos una persona **que conozca** el oficio	*We want a person who knows the trade*

The subjunctive is always used after certain subordinators, for example:

para que (*so that*)

La invitaré para que la **veas**	*I'll invite her so that you may see her*

en caso de que (*in case*)

En caso de que **llegue** dile que me espere	*In case he/she arrives tell him/her to wait*

con tal de que (*as long as*)

Te lo contaré con tal de que no se lo **digas**	*I'll tell you as long as you don't tell him/her*

The subjunctive is found in main clauses containing commands or instructions (imperative form):

Venga aquí un momento, por favor	*Come here a moment, please*
No se lo **diga**	*Don't tell him/her*

The idea of unreality or something which has not yet taken place is a common feature of many subjunctive clauses:

Se lo diré cuando **llegue** — *I'll tell him/her when he/she arrives*

Trabajaré hasta que **termine** — *I'll work until I finish*

For other uses of the subjunctive see Units 22 and 23.

2 Present subjunctive

Uses

The uses of the present subjunctive are no different from those of the subjunctive in general, as outlined earlier. The decision whether to use the present rather than some other subjunctive tense will depend largely on tense agreement and time reference. Although there is no strict rule about it, the present subjunctive normally occurs in sentences which carry a main clause in the present indicative, future or imperative.

Present indicative → present subjunctive
No creo que él esté allí — *I don't think he's there*

Future → present subjunctive
Será imposible que ellos nos visiten — *It'll be impossible for them to visit us*

Imperative → present subjunctive
Alégrate de que no sea nada serio — *You should be glad it's nothing serious* (literally, *be glad ...*)

Formation

Like the imperative (see Unit 20) the present subjunctive is formed from the 1st person singular of the present indicative, e.g. **hablo** (**hablar**, *to speak*), **respondo** (**responder**, *to reply, answer*) **escribo** (**escribir**, *to write*). Drop the **-o** and add the corresponding endings: one set of endings for 1st conjugation verbs and another for the 2nd and 3rd conjugation. The 1st and 3rd person singular of the present subjunctive correspond in form to formal imperatives (see Unit 20).

hablar (*to speak*)	**responder** (*to reply*)	**escribir** (*to write*)
hable	responda	escriba
hables	respondas	escribas
hable	responda	escriba
hablemos	respondamos	escribamos
habléis	respondáis	escribáis
hablen	respondan	escriban

Study the use of the present subjunctive in the following sentences:

- With verbs expressing emotion:

Espero que ellos **hablen** español	*I hope they speak Spanish*
Me alegro de que ellos **trabajen** tan bien juntos	*I'm glad they work so well together*
Temo que ella no **comprenda**	*I'm afraid she may not understand*

- With phrases indicating possibility:

Es posible que ellos no **respondan**	*It's possible that they may not answer*
Es probable que él nos **escriba**	*He'll probably write to us*
Puede ser que **regresen** en avión	*They may return by plane*

- With verbs indicating doubt or uncertainty:

Dudamos que él nos **responda**	*We doubt that he will reply to us*
No creo que Carlos me **escriba**	*I don't think Carlos will write to me*

- In independent clauses with words indicating doubt and possibility:

Quizás John **hable** con él mañana	*Perhaps John will speak to him tomorrow*
Tal vez ella **viaje** a Inglaterra	*Perhaps she may travel to England*
Posiblemente se **queden** allí	*They may stay there*

If the clause with **creer** is in the affirmative, the verb in the subordinate clause will be an indicative verb. Compare these two sentences:

No creo que él me **llame**	*I don't think he'll call me*
Creo que él me **llamará**	*I think he'll call me*

Irregular forms of the present subjunctive

As with imperatives, verbs which are irregular in the 1st person singular of the present indicative are also irregular in the present subjunctive. Overleaf is an example:

Infinitive	Present indicative	Present subjunctive
		1st person
decir (*to say, tell*)	digo	diga
		digas
		diga
		digamos
		digáis
		digan

For other examples of irregular forms refer to irregular imperatives in Unit 20.

As was the case with imperatives, some verbs are irregular in a different way:

dar (*to give*)	dé, des, dé
	demos, deis, den
estar (*to be*)	esté, estés, esté,
	estemos, estéis, estén
haber (*to have*, aux.)	haya, hayas, haya,
	hayamos, hayáis, hayan
ir (*to go*)	vaya, vayas, vaya,
	vayamos, vayáis, vayan
saber (*to know*)	sepa, sepas, sepa,
	sepamos, sepáis, sepan
ser (*to be*)	sea, seas, sea,
	seamos, seáis, sean

The 1st and 3rd person singular of **dar** must carry an accent in order to distinguish them from the preposition **de**. The accents in the present subjunctive of **estar** are the same as in the present indicative: está, está, estáis, están.

Me alegro de que me lo **digas**	*I'm glad you're telling me*
Temo que él no lo **haga** bien	*I'm afraid he may not do it well*
Esperamos que ella lo **tenga**	*We hope she has it*
Dudo que Pedro **esté** allí	*I doubt that Pedro is there*
No creo que Enrique **vaya** a Granada	*I don't think Enrique will go to Granada*
Es posible que Elena **sepa** dónde está Carlos	*It's possible that Elena may know where Carlos is*
Espero que **sea** posible	*I hope it's possible*

3 Verbs and phrases denoting emotion

Here is a list of verbs and phrases denoting emotion, which require the use of the subjunctive in the subordinate clause:

alegrarse	*to be glad*
esperar	*to hope*
importar	*to mind*
molestarse	*to be annoyed*
sentir (e→ie)	*to be sorry*
sorprenderse	*to be surprised*
temer	*to fear*
es una lástima	*it's a pity*
es una pena	*it's a pity*
es una vergüenza	*it's a shame*
¡qué pena …!	*what a pity!*
¡qué lástima …!	*what a pity!*
¡qué vergüenza …!	*what a shame!*
¡qué rabia …!	*what a nuisance!*

Me **sorprende** que digas eso	*I'm surprised you say that*
No me **importa** que él se marche	*I don't mind if he leaves*
Es **una vergüenza** que hagas eso	*It's a shame you did that*
¡**Qué rabia** que él no hable español!	*What a nuisance that he doesn't speak Spanish!*

4 Subjunctive or indicative

Some words and phrases associated with the expression of possibility and doubt may be used equally with the indicative or the subjunctive, for example:

Quizá(s) él habla/hable español	*Perhaps he speaks Spanish*
Tal vez ella sabe/sepa la verdad	*Perhaps she knows the truth*

But note that when **quizá(s)** or **tal vez** come after the verb, this must be in the indicative form:

Él habla español **quizá(s)**	*He speaks Spanish perhaps*
Ella sabe la verdad **tal vez**	*She knows the truth perhaps*

A lo mejor, *perhaps*, is always used with an indicative verb:

A lo mejor vienen/nos invitan *Perhaps they'll come/invite us*

Posiblemente, *possibly*, is normally used with the subjunctive, but it also accepts the indicative:

Posiblemente está/esté allí   *He's possibly there*

5 Expressing emotional reactions, possibility and doubt with reference to the recent past

To express ideas such as *I hope he has found it*, *I don't think they have seen me*, you need to use a present indicative verb in the main clause followed by a verb in the perfect subjunctive in the subordinate clause.

Perfect subjunctive

The perfect subjunctive is formed with the present subjunctive of **haber**, *to have* (**haya, hayas, haya, hayamos, hayáis, hayan**), followed by a past participle:

Espero que él lo **haya**   *I hope he has found it*
    encontrado
No creo que me **hayan visto**   *I don't think they have seen me*

In context

1 An invitation to a birthday party.

Felipe   Hola José Luis. Quiero invitarte a casa esta noche. Es el cumpleaños de Paloma.

José Luis Lo siento, Felipe, pero no creo que pueda ir. Hoy llegan mis padres de Tenerife y tendré que ir al aeropuerto a buscarlos.

Felipe   Es una lástima que no puedas venir. Posiblemente venga Francisco. Está en Madrid.

José Luis Me alegro de que esté otra vez aquí. Espero verlo otro día. Dile que me llame.

Felipe   Se lo diré. ¿Estarás en casa mañana?

José Luis Tal vez salga un par de horas por la mañana, pero volveré antes del mediodía.

Felipe   Vale. Le diré a Francisco que te llame por la tarde.

José Luis De acuerdo. Gracias.

es una lástima	*it's a pity*
otro día	*another day*
un par de horas	*a couple of hours*

2 Read this extract from a letter

Querida Jane

Hemos recibido tu carta y nos alegramos de que estés bien y tengas tanto éxito en tus estudios. Sentimos mucho que no puedas venir a Barcelona el próximo verano, pero esperamos que vengas para las Navidades. Es posible que Gonzalo también pase las Navidades con nosotros. ¿Te acuerdas de él? Es aquel chico guapo que conocimos en Blanes ...

tanto éxito	so much success
¿te acuerdas de él?	do you remember him?
que conocimos (conocer)	that we met (to meet, get to know)

Practice

1 Read this letter sent to Paul by a Spanish-speaking friend and change the infinitives in brackets into the appropriate form.

Querido Paul

¡Hace tanto tiempo que no sé nada de ti! Espero que (1) (recibir, tú) la carta que te envié hace dos meses, en la que te decía que es muy probable que este verano (2) (ir, yo) a verte. No creo que (3) (quedarse, yo) mucho tiempo, pero creo que (4) (estar, yo) contigo por lo menos dos semanas. ¿Qué te parece?

Lola me contó que habías encontrado trabajo en un colegio. Me alegro mucho de que (5) (conseguir, tú) lo que buscabas, y espero que (6) (estar, tú) contento allí y que el colegio te (7) (pagar) bien. A mí no me gusta mucho lo que hago, pero dudo que (8) (encontrar, yo) algo mejor. No es nada fácil ...

2 You and a Spanish-speaking friend are exchanging news about people you have not seen for a long time. Use the phrases in brackets to express your feelings about the news you hear. Follow the example.

Ejemplo ¿Sabes que Antonio se casa? (alegrarse)
   Me alegro de que se case.

a ¿Sabes que Cristina se divorcia? (es una lástima)
b Alfredo vuelve a España. (alegrarse)
c Laura no seguirá estudiando. (¡qué pena!)

d Pepe y Paca van a comprar una casa. (alegrarse)
e Mario está enfermo. (sentir)
f Cristóbal espera ir a Nueva York. (esperar)
g Mariana deja su trabajo. (sorprenderse)
h María y Lola se van de Madrid. (¡qué lástima!)

3 Choose a suitable caption for each picture from the phrases below.

a Me encanta que me regalen flores.
b Es probable que la reparación sea un poco cara. Está en muy malas condiciones.
c Espero que hoy esté Vd. mejor.
d Espero que con esto me deje tranquilo.

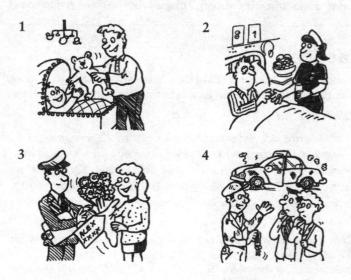

22

expressing wishes and orders

In this unit you will learn how to
- express wishes and preferences involving others
- express orders in an indirect way

Language points
- imperfect subjunctive
- conditional tense
- verbs and phrases denoting wishes and preferences

Key sentences

Wishes and preferences involving other people and indirect orders, such as *He wants me to help him*, **Quiere que le (or lo) ayude**, *I want you to go*, **Quiero que vayas**, are expressed in Spanish with a subjunctive verb in the subordinate clause.

In the previous sentences, the main verb is in the present indicative tense, so the verb in the subordinate clause is in the present subjunctive. But if reference is to the past, as in *He wanted me to help him, I wanted you to go*, the verb in the subordinate clause must in Spanish be in the imperfect subjunctive, not the present. This new tense of the subjunctive as well as the conditional tense are illustrated in the examples and explained in the grammar notes which follow.

Expressing wishes and preferences involving others

Quiero que me llames/ escribas	*I want you to call me/write to me*
Quería que me llamaras/ escribieras	*I wanted you to call me/write to me*
¿Qué quieres que haga/diga?	*What do you want me to do/say?*
¿Qué querías que hiciera/ dijera?	*What did you want me to do/say?*
Prefiero que esperes/te quedes aquí	*I prefer you to wait/stay here*
Preferiría que esperaras/te quedaras aquí	*I'd prefer you to wait/stay here*
Me gustaría que estudiara/ aprendiera español	*I'd like him/her to study/learn Spanish*

Expressing indirect orders

Les he ordenado/exigido que trabajen más	*I have ordered them to work more*
Les ordené/exigí que trabajaran más	*I ordered them to work more*
Te estoy diciendo que no lo repitas	*I'm telling you not to repeat it*
Te dije que no lo repitieras	*I told you not to repeat it*

Grammar summary

1 Imperfect subjunctive

Uses

The imperfect subjunctive normally occurs in sentences which carry a main clause in the imperfect, preterite or pluperfect, or else in the conditional (see 2 on page 161) or the conditional perfect (see Unit 23). Here are some examples:

Imperfect indicative → imperfect subjunctive
Yo no quería que él **se**   *I didn't want him to leave*
  marchara

Preterite → imperfect subjunctive
Él no quiso que yo lo   *He didn't want me to take*
  llevara   *him*

Pluperfect indicative → imperfect subjunctive
Ella nos había pedido que la   *She had asked us to call her*
  llamáramos

Conditional → imperfect subjunctive
Yo preferiría que os **quedarais**   *I'd prefer you to stay*

Conditional perfect → imperfect subjunctive
Yo habría preferido que   *I'd have preferred you to stay*
  os **quedarais**

Formation

The imperfect subjunctive can be formed in two ways. The first is directly derived from the 3rd person plural of the preterite (see Unit 18). Here are some examples with regular verbs:

Infinitive		Preterite (3rd person pl.)	Imperfect subjunctive (1st and 3rd person sing.)
llegar	(*to arrive*)	llegaron	llegara
beber	(*to drink*)	bebieron	bebiera
subir	(*to go up*)	subieron	subiera

The same derivation occurs with irregular and stem-changing verbs.

poder	(*to be able to*)	pudieron	pudiera
estar	(*to be*)	estuvieron	estuviera
decir	(*to say*)	dijeron	dijera
ir/ser	(*to go/to be*)	fueron	fuera
traer	(*to bring*)	trajeron	trajera

Here is the imperfect subjunctive of three regular verbs representing each of the three conjugations: **llegar** (*to arrive*), **beber** (*to drink*) and **subir** (*to go up*). Note that -er and -ir verbs share the same endings:

llegar	beber	subir
llegara	bebiera	subiera
llegaras	bebieras	subieras
llegara	bebiera	subiera
llegáramos	bebiéramos	subiéramos
llegarais	bebierais	subierais
llegaran	bebieran	subieran

The imperfect subjunctive has a second set of endings which appear to be less frequent than the first. The two forms are generally interchangeable. Again, -er and -ir verbs share the same endings:

llegar	beber	subir
llegase	bebiese	subiese
llegases	bebieses	subieses
llegase	bebiese	subiese
llegásemos	bebiésemos	subiésemos
llegaseis	bebieseis	subieseis
llegasen	bebiesen	subiesen

Expressing wishes and preferences involving others

Él quería que yo **llegara/ llegase** a la hora
He wanted me to arrive on time

Ella prefería que yo no **bebiera/bebiese**
She preferred me not to drink

Roberto no deseaba que tú **fueras/fueses**
Roberto didn't want you to go

Yo quería que nos **quedáramos/quedásemos**
I wanted us to stay

Expressing orders in an indirect way

Nos ordenó que **llegáramos/ llegásemos** a la hora
He ordered us to arrive on time

Les ordené que **subieran/ subiesen**
I ordered them to go up

El jefe me exigió que **trabajara/trabajase** hasta las 6.00
The boss ordered me to work until 6.00

2 Conditional tense

Uses

The conditional tense is often used in sentences which express a wish or preference of some sort, for example:

Me **gustaría** que me escribieras/escribieses	*I'd like you to write to me*
Yo **preferiría** que él no viniera/viniese	*I'd prefer him not to come*

It is also generally used with verbs which express emotion (see Unit 21), for example:

Sentiría que ella no viniera/viniese	*I'd be sorry if she didn't come*
Me **alegraría** de que lo hicieras/hicieses	*I'd be glad if you did it*
Sería una lástima que no la encontráramos	*It would be a pity if we didn't find her*

Formation

Like the future tense, the conditional is formed with the infinitive, to which the endings are added. The endings of the three conjugations are the same as those of the imperfect tense of -**er** and -**ir** verbs (see Unit 19). Here is the conditional tense of a regular verb:

preferir (*to prefer*)	
preferiría	*I'd prefer*
preferirías	*you'd prefer* (fam.)
preferiría	*you/he/she would prefer*
preferiríamos	*we would prefer*
preferiríais	*you would prefer* (fam.)
preferirían	*you/they would prefer*

The endings are exactly the same for -**ar** and -**er** verbs.

Preferiría que no fueras/fueses a Bogotá	*I'd prefer you not to go to Bogota*
Me **gustaría** que nos encontráramos/encontrásemos en España	*I'd like us to meet in Spain*
Nos **gustaría** que tú nos acompañaras/acompañases	*We'd like you to accompany us*

Irregular conditional forms

Verbs which have irregular stems in the future tense (see Unit 15) also have them in the conditional. The endings are the same as those of regular verbs. Here are some of the most common.

decir (*to say*)	diría, dirías, diría, diríamos, diríais, dirían
haber (*to have* (aux.))	habría, habrías, habría, habríamos, habríais, habrían
hacer (*to do, make*)	haría, harías, haría, haríamos, haríais, harían
poder (*can, to be able*)	podría, podrías, podría, podríamos, podríais, podrían
poner (*to put*)	pondría, pondrías, pondría, pondríamos, pondríais, pondrían
querer (*to want*)	querría, querrías, querría, querríamos, querríais, querrían
saber (*to know*)	sabría, sabrías, sabría, sabríamos, sabríais, sabrían
salir (*to go out*)	saldría, saldrías, saldría, saldríamos, saldríais, saldrían
tener (*to have*)	tendría, tendrías, tendría, tendríamos, tendríais, tendrían
venir (*to come*)	vendría, vendrías, vendría, vendríamos, vendríais, vendrían

For a list of the most common irregular verbs in all tenses see pages 203–6.

Yo no **querría** que él se marchara/marchase	*I wouldn't want him to leave*
Yo no **sabría** qué hacer	*I wouldn't know what to do*
Tú **tendrías** que trabajar más	*You'd have to work more*
¿Qué **haríamos** sin ti?	*What would we do without you?*

Because of the meaning of these irregular verbs, some of the examples do not correspond to the expression of wishes and indirect orders.

3 Verbs and phrases denoting wishes and preferences

The verbs most commonly associated with the expression of wishes and preferences are **querer**, *to want*, **gustar**, *to like*,

preferir, *to prefer*. Other less frequent words and expressions are the following: **agradar**, *to like*, **desear**, *to wish*, **encantar**, *to like very much*, *to love*, **sería bueno/estupendo/magnífico**, *it would be good/great.*

Agradar and **desear** are used in more formal contexts, especially in the written language:

Me **agradaría** mucho que nos visitara	*I'd very much like you to visit us*
Desearía que me respondiera lo antes posible	*I should like you to answer me as soon as possible*
Me **encantaría** que pasaras tus vacaciones conmigo	*I'd very much like you to spend your holidays with me*
Sería estupendo que nevara.	*It would be great if it snowed*

Note that **agradar** and **encantar** are conjugated like **gustar**.

In context

1 An invitation to the cinema.

Antonio Sara, me gustaría que me acompañaras al cine esta noche. Hay una película estupenda en el cine Capri.

Sara Me encantaría ir contigo, pero desgraciadamente no puedo. Javier me pidió que fuera a su casa esta noche. Si no te importa, preferiría que lo dejáramos para mañana.

Antonio De acuerdo. Hasta mañana, entonces.

me encantaría	*I'd love to*
si no te importa	*if you don't mind*
preferiría que lo dejáramos	*I'd prefer if we left it*

2 Read this extract from a letter.

Querida Soledad

Cristóbal me pidió que te escribiera para reiterarte nuestra invitación para este verano. Nos gustaría mucho que pasaras estas vacaciones con nosotros. Podríamos ir a Viña del Mar, como lo hicimos la última vez que estuviste en Chile. ¿Te gustaría?

Mi jefe me ha dicho que tome mis vacaciones a partir del 15 de enero, de manera que si estás libre entonces puedes venirte de inmediato. Preferiría que me lo confirmaras lo antes posible para hacer las reservas de hotel. ¿Qué te parece?

como lo hicimos	*as we did*
la última vez	*last time*
a partir de	*starting on*
lo antes posible	*as soon as possible*

Note that the sentence **Javier me pidió que fuera a su casa,** *Javier asked me to go to his house* – denoting an indirect request – is grammatically the same as sentences such as:

| Javier quería que fuera a su casa | *Javier wanted me to go to his house* |
| Javier me ordenó que fuera a su casa | *Javier ordered me to go to his house* |

The three sentences only differ in their meaning or function. In the second text observe also the sentence:

| Cristóbal me pidió que te escribiera | *Cristóbal asked me to write to you* |

Practice

1 Simón and Lola never seem to agree in their wishes and preferences. Use the phrases in brackets to complete Lola's replies to Simón's statements. Follow the example.

Ejemplo Me gustaría que pasáramos las vacaciones en Italia.
(Prefiero que … en Francia)
Prefiero que las pasemos en Francia.

a Me gustaría que fuéramos en avión. (Prefiero que … en el coche)
b Quiero que nos quedemos en un camping. (Me gustaría que … en un hotel)
c Prefiero que salgamos el viernes. (Preferiría que … el sábado)
d Quiero que invitemos a mi madre. (Preferiría que no la…)
e Me encantaría que Paco viniera con nosotros. (Prefiero que … Julio)
f Sería mejor que tú hicieras la reserva. (Prefiero que … tú mismo)

2 Felipe has been away from the office for a couple of days. On his return he found the following note from a colleague. Change the infinitives in brackets into the appropriate form.

Felipe

Ayer llamó el señor Parker de Inglaterra y me pidió que te (1) (informar, yo) que no podrá viajar el día 30 como tenía planeado. Quiere que tú lo/le (2) (llamar) esta tarde para fijar una nueva fecha. También llamaron de la empresa Grasco y me pidieron que te (3) (recordar, yo) que todavía no han recibido el pedido. Quieren que se lo (4) (enviar, tú) lo antes posible.

El gerente quiere que (5) (pasar, tú) por su despacho y le (6) (llevar, tú) el informe que te pidió.

Isabel

3 Match each picture with a suitable caption from the sentences below.

a Me gustaría que Luis aprendiera a tocar la guitarra.
b No me gustaría que mi novio hiciera el servicio militar.
c Preferiría que no condujera tan rápido.
d Creo que sería mejor que viajáramos en avión.
e Nos gustaría mucho que nuestro hijo fuera médico.
f Me encantaría que me escribieras un poema.

23

expressing conditions

In this unit you will learn how to
- express open conditions
- express remote conditions
- express unfulfilled conditions

Language points
- *si* in conditional sentences
- pluperfect subjunctive
- conditional perfect
- pluperfect subjunctive for conditional perfect in unfulfilled conditions
- phrases expressing conditions

Key sentences

Conditions may be expressed in English through the word *if*, in constructions such as the following: *If I have time I'll go, If I had time I'd go, If I'd had time I'd have gone.* Look at the following sentences and their translations and then read the grammar notes which follow for an explanation of how these ideas are expressed in Spanish.

Expressing open conditions

Si tengo tiempo iré   *If I have time I'll go*
Si ella viene/me lo pregunta   *If she comes/asks me*
  se lo diré/contaré   *I'll tell her*

Expressing remote conditions

Si tuviera/tuviese tiempo iría. *If I had time I'd go*
Si me llamara/llamase   *If she called me*
  la invitaría   *I'd invite her*

Expressing unfulfilled conditions

Si yo hubiera/hubiese tenido *If I'd had time I'd have*
  tiempo habría ido   *gone*
Si hubiéramos/hubiésemos   *If we'd known we'd have*
  sabido habríamos venido   *come*

Grammar summary

1 *Si* (if) in conditional sentences

In open conditions

Si is the word most frequently used in Spanish when we want to express conditions. In open conditions, that is, conditions which may or may not be fulfilled, si is always followed by an indicative tense, with a tense pattern which is no different from English. Consider these examples and, again, the ones under Key sentences:

Si es como él dice es mejor   *If it is as he says it's better not*
  no hacerlo (si + present +   *to do it*
  present)

Si ella me escribe le responderé de inmediato (**si** + present + future)	*If she writes to me I'll answer her right away*
Si has hecho tus deberes podrás salir (**si** + perfect tense + future)	*If you've done your homework you'll be able to go out*
Si salieron a las 6.00 ya deben de estar en Caracas (**si** + preterite + present)	*If they left at 6.00 they must already be in Caracas*

In remote conditions

In remote conditions such as **si lloviera/lloviese no saldríamos** (*if it rained we wouldn't go out*), the **si** clause carries a verb in the imperfect subjunctive (see Unit 22) followed by a clause with a verb in the conditional. Here are some examples:

Imperfect subjunctive + conditional

Si fueras/fueses allí la verías	*If you went there you'd see her*
Si tomáramos/tomásemos un taxi llegaríamos a tiempo	*If we took a taxi we'd arrive on time*

The latter two examples correspond to conditions which may be fulfilled. There is little difference between these conditions and the ones expressed in:

Si vas allí la verás	*If you go there you'll see her*
Si tomamos un taxi llegaremos a tiempo	*If we take a taxi we'll arrive on time*

Now consider these examples:

Si ella hablara/hablase inglés la contrataríamos	*If she spoke English we'd hire her*
Si él estuviera/estuviese aquí te lo presentaría	*If he were here I'd introduce him to you*

These last examples correspond to conditions which are contrary to fact:

ella no habla inglés	*she doesn't speak English*
él no está aquí	*he's not here*

The verb in the **si** clause here must necessarily be in the subjunctive.

Unfulfilled conditions

In unfulfilled conditions such as **si hubiera/hubiese llovido no habríamos salido** (*if it had rained we wouldn't have gone out*), the **si** clause carries a verb in the pluperfect subjunctive followed by a clause with a verb in the perfect conditional:

Si ellos se hubieran/hubiesen   *If they had married they'd*
  casado habrían sido felices   *have been happy*
Si Miguel me hubiera/hubiese   *If Miguel had invited me I'd*
  invitado yo habría aceptado   *have accepted*

For the formation of the pluperfect subjunctive and the conditional perfect and further examples of conditional sentences see paras. 2 and 3 below.

2 Pluperfect subjunctive

Usage

Apart from its specific use in unfulfilled conditions, the uses of the pluperfect subjunctive are, generally speaking, those of the subjunctive as a whole. It is normally found in subordinate clauses preceded by a main clause with a verb in the past, for example:

No creí que él hubiera   *I didn't think he had*
  tenido éxito   *succeeded*

But note further:

Creí que él había tenido éxito   *I thought he had succeeded*

Formation

The pluperfect subjunctive is formed with the imperfect subjunctive of **haber** plus a past participle. Example:

	hubiera/hubiese ido			I had gone
	hubieras/hubieses ido			you had gone (fam.)
Si	hubiera/hubiese ido		If	you/he/she had gone
	hubiéramos/hubiésemos ido			we had gone
	hubierais/hubieseis ido			you had gone (fam.)
	hubieran/hubiesen ido			you/they had gone

The two endings are interchangeable.

Si hubieras/hubieses ido a   *If you had gone to Seville*
  Sevilla te habría gustado   *you'd have liked it*
Si ellos hubieran/hubiesen   *If they had had money*
  tenido dinero habrían viajado   *they'd have travelled*

3 Conditional perfect

Usage

The most common use of the conditional perfect is in sentences which refer to actions which could have taken place under certain conditions, as in *If I had known he was here, I wouldn't have come.*

Formation

The conditional perfect is formed with the conditional of **haber** followed by a past participle:

habría estudiado	*I would have studied*
habrías estudiado	*you would have studied* (fam.)
habría estudiado	*you/he/she would have studied*
habríamos estudiado	*we would have studied*
habríais estudiado	*you would have studied* (fam.)
habrían estudiado	*you/they would have studied*

Si yo hubiera/hubiese tenido el libro habría estudiado	*If I had had the book I would have studied*
Si ella hubiera/hubiese visto la película le habría gustado	*If she had seen the film she would have liked it*
Si hubiéramos/hubiésemos podido te habríamos ayudado	*If we had been able to we would have helped you*

4 Pluperfect subjunctive for conditional perfect in unfulfilled conditions

In colloquial speech the conditional perfect is sometimes replaced by the pluperfect subjunctive (the **-ra** form). The result is that you get the same tense in the **si** clause and in the main clause. Here are some examples:

Si yo no hubiera/hubiese comido ese pescado no me hubiera (habría) enfermado	*If I hadn't eaten that fish I wouldn't have become ill*
Si Juan hubiera/hubiese sabido lo que pasó se hubiera (habría) enfadado	*If Juan had known what happened he would have got angry*

5 Phrases expressing conditions

a menos que, a no ser que (*unless*):

No vendré mañana, **a menos que/a no ser que** tú me lo pidas — *I won't come tomorrow unless you ask me to*

a condición de que, con tal (de) que (*as long as*):

Te lo contaré **a condición de que/con tal (de) que** no se lo digas a nadie — *I'll tell you as long as you don't tell anybody*

por si (*in case*), **por si acaso** (*just in case*):

He comprado más carne **por si** José viene a cenar — *I've bought more meat in case José comes to dinner*

Cambiaré más dinero **por si acaso** — *I'll change some more money just in case*

In context

1 If I had known …

Ricardo ¿Sabes que Julia estuvo aquí ayer?

Gonzalo ¡Qué lástima! Si lo hubiera sabido habría venido yo también. Hace mucho tiempo que no la veo.

Ricardo Ahora está en casa de sus padres. Si quieres podemos llamarla.

Gonzalo De acuerdo.

2 If I had money …

Edgardo Alba ha decidido vender su piso. ¿Lo sabías?

Mónica ¡No me digas! Es un piso estupendo. Si tuviera dinero lo compraría. ¿Sabes en cuánto lo vende?

Edgardo No lo sé, pero si te interesa puedo preguntárselo.

Mónica Sí, me interesa mucho. Es un piso muy bonito y es bastante grande.

Edgardo Se lo preguntaré.

ha decidido (decidir)	*she has decided*
¡no me digas!	*don't say*

Practice

1 Can you make sense of these conditions? Match each phrase on the left with a suitable phrase from the right.

a Si hubiera tenido dinero ...   1 la invitaré a la fiesta.
b Si tuviera tiempo ...   2 le darían el puesto.
c Si veo a Ángeles ...   3 los hubiera esperado.
d Si lloviera ...   4 te lo habría prestado.
e Si hubiese sabido que   5 te ayudaría.
  vendrían ...   6 nos quedaríamos en casa.
f Si hablara mejor español ...

2 Your friend Helen has received an invitation from someone in Spain, and as her Spanish is not very good she has asked you to translate the following reply for her.

Dear Mari Carmen,

Thanks for your letter and your invitation to visit you in Spain. Unfortunately, I have to work all summer, but if I were free I'd certainly visit you. I'd love to see you again. Perhaps at Christmas, if I can, unless you want to come and stay with me then. It would be great!

I'm glad you've found a job. I know it's not what you wanted, but it's a job. I'd have taken it too. I hope you like it.

3 A group of people were asked what they would do if they won a big lottery prize. What were their answers? Match the drawings opposite with the phrases below and put the verbs in the correct form, following the example.

Ejemplo: Si (ganar) la lotería, (yo) (dejar) mi trabajo y (dedicarse) a viajar.
Si ganara la lotería, dejaría mi trabajo y me dedicaría a viajar.

Si ganara la lotería...
1 ... (yo) (construir) una gran casa junto al mar.
2 ... mi familia y yo (comprar) un yate y (dar) la vuelta al mundo.
3 ... mi mujer y yo (cambiar) nuestros coches/carros (L. Am.)
4 ... mi novio y yo (ir) de vacaciones a la montaña y (aprender) a esquiar.
5 ... mi familia y yo (hacer) una gran fiesta e (invitar) a todos nuestros amigos.
6 ... mi vida no (cambiar) mucho y (seguir) trabajando igual.

congratulations

Congratulations on completing *Teach Yourself Spanish Grammar*!

We hope you have enjoyed working your way through the course. We are always keen to receive feedback from people who have used our course, so why not contact us and let us know your reactions? We'll be particularly pleased to receive your praise, but we should also like to know if things could be improved. We always welcome comments and suggestions, and we do our best to incorporate constructive suggestions into later editions.

You can contact us through the publishers at:
Teach Yourself Books, Hodder Headline Ltd, 338 Euston Road, London NW1 3BH, UK.

We hope you will want to build on your knowledge of Spanish and we have made a few suggestions to help you do this in the section entitled **Taking it further**, on page 207.

¡Buena suerte!
Juan Kattán-Ibarra

adjectives Adjectives are words used to describe nouns, e.g. The house is very *comfortable*. **La casa es muy cómoda.**

adverbs Adverbs provide more information about verbs, adjectives or other adverbs, e.g. She spoke *slowly*. **Habló pausadamente.** It's *absolutely* necessary. **Es absolutamente necesario.** They behaved *incredibly* well. **Se comportaron increíblemente bien.**

articles There are two types of articles, *definite* and *indefinite*. Definite articles are **el, la, los** and **las,** *the* in English. Indefinite articles are **un** and **una,** *a* in English and **unos, unas,** *some*.

clause In a sentence such as *I hope that they come*, **Espero que vengan,** there are two clauses: a main clause *I hope*, **Espero,** and a subordinate clause *that they come*, **que vengan.**

demonstratives Demonstratives are words like *this*, **este, esta,** *that*, **ese, esa,** *these*, **estos, estas,** *those*, **esos, esas.**

gender There are two genders in Spanish, masculine and feminine. All nouns are, therefore, either masculine or feminine, e.g. **la casa,** *house*, feminine, **el coche,** *car*, masculine.

gerund Words such as *speaking*, **hablando,** *drinking*, **bebiendo,** are known as gerunds.

imperative The imperative is the form of the verb that is used to give directions, instructions, orders or commands, e.g. *Go straight on*. **Siga todo recto.** *Put it here*. **Póngalo aquí.**

infinitive This is the basic form of the verb, as found in the dictionary, e.g. *to speak*, **hablar,** *to answer*, **responder.**

nouns Nouns are words like *book*, **libro**, *difficulty*, **dificultad**.

number This word is used to indicate whether something is *singular* or *plural*.

object This is that part of the sentence which undergoes the action expressed by the verb. In a sentence such as *He sold the car to Maria*, **Vendió el coche a María**, *the car*, **el coche**, is said to be the *direct object*, because the car is what was sold. María, the recipient, is the *indirect object*.

past participle A past participle is that part of the verb which is used in compound tenses, e.g. *I have finished*. **He terminado**. *They had returned*. **Habían vuelto**. *Finished*, **terminado**, and *returned*, **vuelto**, are the past participles.

personal pronouns These are words such as *I*, **yo**, *he*, **él**, *she*, **ella**, *we*, **nosotros/as**.

possessives Words like *my*, **mi**, *mine*, **mío**, *your*, **tu**, **su**, *yours*, **tuyo**, **suyo**, are called possessives.

prepositions These are words such as *with*, **con**, *in, on, at*, **en**, *for*, **para**, **por**, *from*, **de**, **desde**.

pronouns Pronouns are words which stand in place of nouns or noun phrases which have already been mentioned, e.g. *My friend Gloria* (noun) *is Spanish. She* (pronoun) *lives in Madrid*. **Mi amiga Gloria es española. Ella vive en Madrid**.

reflexive In a sentence such as *He washed himself*, **Se lavó**, the verb is said to be reflexive because the subject and object are one and the same. Words such as *myself*, **me**, *himself, herself*, **se**, *ourselves*, **nos**, are called *reflexive pronouns*.

subject In a sentence such as *Patricia bought the house*, **Patricia compró la casa**, Patricia is the subject of the verb *to buy*, **comprar**, because it was she who bought the house.

subjunctive mood In a sentence such as *If I were you*, **Yo en tu lugar**, the verb *to be* is said to be in the subjunctive mood. The subjunctive is not used much in English nowadays, but it is common in Spanish.

tense Tenses are forms of the verb which indicate aspects of time, e.g. past, present, future.

verbs Words such as *to go*, **ir**, *to arrive*, **llegar**, *to eat*, **comer**, are called verbs.

This grammar reference section brings together the main grammatical points studied in the units and expands on some of them. It also deals with others which have not been covered.

1 Articles

Definite and indefinite articles (*the, a/an*)

a The word for *the* for singular nouns is **el** for masculine and **la** for feminine, e.g. **el hotel, la habitación**. The plural forms are **los** and **las**, e.g. **los hoteles, las habitaciones**.

b A + **el** becomes **al**, e.g. **Voy** *al* **cine**, and **de** + **el** becomes **del**, e.g. **Vengo** *del* **supermercado**.

c The word for *a/an* is **un** for masculine and **una** for feminine, e.g. **un** señor, **una** señora. The plural forms **unos, unas** mean *some*.

Use of the definite article

a Before nouns used in a general sense, e.g. *los* animales.

b Before an abstract noun, e.g. *la* dificultad.

c Before people's names when they are preceded by a noun or an adjective, e.g. *la* señora García, *el* pobre Carlos.

d Before names of languages, unless they are preceded by the verb **hablar** or the preposition **en**, e.g. **Me gusta** *el* **español**.

e Before the names of certain countries, although the general tendency nowadays is to omit it, e.g. *la* Argentina, *el* Brasil, *el* Perú, *los* Estados Unidos.

f Before names of substances and food, e.g. *el* pescado.

g Before subjects, sports, arts, sciences and illnesses, e.g. *las* matemáticas, *el* tenis, *la* literatura, *la* física, *el* cáncer.

h   Before names of drinks and meals, e.g. *el* café, *la* cena.
i   Before colours, e.g. *el* negro.
j   Before parts of the body, e.g. *las* manos.
k   Before days of the week and other expressions of time, e.g.
    el sábado, *el* 23 de julio, *la* semana pasada.
l   Before words indicating measure and weight, e.g. diez euros
    el kilo.
m   As a substitute for a noun, e.g. *La casa* de María es grande
    y *la* de José también.

Omission of the indefinite article

a   Before words for occupations and professions, nationality,
    religion, e.g. Soy *estudiante/americano*.
b   In certain set phrases which carry the verb tener, e.g. No
    tengo coche/teléfono.
c   Before words like cien, mil, otro, e.g. Tengo *cien/mil* euros,
    ¿Tienes *otro*?
d   After words like que *what a...* and tal *such a...*, e.g. ¡Qué
    lástima!, ¡Hicieron *tal* ruido!

The neuter article *lo*

This is used only with certain adjectives, adverbs and whole
sentences, *never* with a noun, for example:

¡No sabes *lo* bonito que es!	*You don't know how beautiful it is!*
Lo mejor es no decir nada.	*The best thing is not to say anything.*
¿Recuerdas *lo* que te dije ayer?	*Do you remember what I told you yesterday?*

2 Nouns

Masculine and feminine

In Spanish, all nouns are either masculine or feminine. It is not
always possible to recognize the gender of nouns, but the
following simple rules may help you to do so.

Masculine nouns

The following endings correspond normally to masculine nouns,
but there are many exceptions.

-o	el trabajo	*work*
-e	el bebé	*baby*
-l	el sol	*sun*
-r	el amor	*love*

| -n | el tren | *train* |
| -s | el mes | *month* |

The following nouns are also masculine:

Nouns referring to males, e.g. **el señor**; mountains, rivers and seas, e.g. **el Pacífico**; days and seasons, e.g. **el verano**; colours, e.g. **el violeta**; substances, e.g. **el metal**; languages, e.g. **el español**.

Feminine nouns

The following endings correspond normally to feminine nouns, but there are exceptions:

-a	la vida	*life*
-ad	la ciudad	*city*
-z	la paz	*peace*
-ción	la nación	*nation*
-sión	la pasión	*passion*
-ud	la juventud	*youth*

Special rules

a To form the feminine of nouns which refer to people you normally change the -o into -a or add an -a to the final consonant, e.g. **el arquitecto, la arquitecta**; **un inglés, una inglesa**.

b Nouns endings in -ista do not change for masculine or feminine, e.g. **el/la dentista**.

c Most nouns which end in -ente are also invariable, e.g. **el/la estudiante**.

d Some nouns have different forms for each sex, e.g. *el* **padre** *father,* *la* **madre** *mother,* *el* **hombre** *man,* *la* **mujer** *woman.*

e Some nouns change meaning according to gender, e.g. *el* **policía** *policeman,* *la* **policía** *police*; *el* **capital** *capital, money,* *la* **capital** *capital city.*

Plural of nouns

a Most nouns form the plural by adding -s, e.g. **la casa, las casas**.

b Nouns which end in a consonant normally add -es, e.g. **el profesor, los profesores**.

c Nouns which end in -z change -z to -c and add -es, e.g. **una vez, dos veces**.

d The masculine plural of some nouns may be used to refer to members of both sexes, e.g. **el padre** *father,* **los padres** *parents*; **el hermano** *brother,* **los hermanos** *brothers and sisters.*

e Some nouns lose their accent in the plural, e.g. **un inglés** *an Englishman*, **unos ingleses** *some English people*.
f Some nouns gain an accent in the plural, e.g. **el joven** *young man*, **los jóvenes** *the young*.

3 Adjectives

Gender and number agreement

Adjectives must agree in gender and number with the noun they describe.

a Adjectives ending in -o change -o to -a with feminine nouns, e.g. **un hotel pequeño, una habitación pequeña**.
b Adjectives that end in a vowel other than -o or -a do not change for feminine, e.g. **una mujer/un hombre inteligente** *an intelligent woman/man*.
c Adjectives that end in a consonant do not normally change for masculine and feminine, e.g. **un vestido azul** *a blue dress*, **una camisa azul** *a blue shirt*.
d Adjectives indicating nationality form the feminine by changing -o into -a or adding -a to the consonant, e.g. **un periódico español** *a Spanish newspaper*, **una revista españo**la *a Spanish magazine*.

To form the plural of adjectives follow the same rules as for nouns (see paragraph 2).

Position of adjectives

a The great majority of adjectives come after the noun, e.g. **una persona** *inteligente*.
b Adjectives are sometimes used before nouns for emphasis or to convey some kind of emotion, e.g. **un** *excelente* **profesor**.
c Certain adjectives, among them **grande, pequeño, bueno, malo**, usually precede the adjective, e.g. **un** *pequeño* **problema**.
d **Grande** normally follows the noun when its meaning is *big* or *large*, but it goes before it when it means *great*. Before the noun, **grande** becomes **gran**, e.g. **una persona** *grande*, **una** *gran* **persona**.
e Like **grande, bueno** *good* and **malo** *bad* have a different form when they come before a noun, e.g. **un libro** *bueno* or **un buen libro** *a good book*; **un día** *malo* or **un** *mal* **día** *a bad day*.

Comparative form of adjectives

Superiority:

Madrid es *más grande* que Barcelona.	Madrid is larger than Barcelona.

Inferiority:

Mi coche es *menos potente* que el tuyo.	My car is less powerful than yours.

Equality:

Mi casa es *tan bonita* como la de ella.	My house is as pretty as hers.

Irregular forms:

bueno	*good*	mejor	*better*
malo	*bad*	peor	*worse*
grande	*big*	mayor/más grande	*bigger*
pequeño	*small*	menor/más pequeño	*smaller*

Superlative form

To express ideas such as *the fastest*, *the most expensive*, use the construction definite article, **el, la, los** or **las**, followed by **más** and the appropriate adjective.

Mi coche es *el más rápido*.	My car is the fastest.
Esta tienda es *la más cara*.	This shop is the most expensive.

To say *the best* or *the worst*, use the definite article followed by the appropriate word, **mejor** or **peor**.

Ésa es *la mejor* solución.	That is the best solution.
Éstos son *los peores*.	These are the worst.

4 Adverbs

a To form an adverb from an adjective, add **-mente** to the singular form of the adjective, e.g. **amable**, **amable*mente***.
b If the adjective ends in **-o**, change the **-o** to **-a** and then add **-mente**, e.g. **rápido**, **rápid*amente***.
c Many adverbs are not derived from adjectives, e.g. **ahora**, **mañana**, **aquí**, **bien**.

5 Pronouns

Subject pronouns

Singular		*Plural*	
yo	*I*	nosotros/as	*we*
tú	*you* (familiar)	vosotros/as	*you* (familiar)
usted	*you* (formal)	ustedes	*you* (plural)
él, ella	*he, she*	ellos, ellas	*they* (masc./fem.)

Vosotros and all forms associated with it are not used in Latin America, where **ustedes** is used in formal and informal address.

Subject pronouns are usually omitted in Spanish, unless you want to add emphasis or to avoid ambiguity.

Direct and indirect object pronouns: 1st and 2nd persons

Object pronouns can be direct, e.g. *La* invité, *I invited her*; or indirect, as in *Le* dije, *I said to her/him/you* (formal).

In the first and second person singular and plural there is no distinction between direct and indirect object pronouns, e.g. *Me* invitó, *He/She invited me*; *Me* dijo, *He/She said to me*.

Singular		*Plural*	
me	*me, to me*	nos	*us, to us*
te	*you, to you* (familiar)	os	*you, to you* (familiar)

In the third person, direct and indirect object pronouns differ, e.g. **Lo** (or **le**) invité (direct), *I invited him*; **Le** dije (indirect), *I said to him/her*. The following are their forms:

Direct object pronouns: 3rd person

Singular		*Plural*	
lo/le	*you* (formal)/*him/it* (m.)	los/les	*you* (formal)/*them* (m.)
la	*you* (formal)/*her/it* (f.)	las	*you* (formal)/*them* (f.)

Le/s, as a direct object, is used by most people in central and northern Spain when talking about human males, e.g. **Le/s llamé**, *I called him/them*, with **lo/s** referring to masculine objects, e.g. **Lo/s compré**, *I bought it/them*. In other parts of Spain and in Latin America as a whole most people use **lo/s** for both human males and masculine objects, e.g. **Lo llamé**, *I called him*; **Lo compré**, *I bought it*. In the feminine there are generally no regional differences. The **lo** form may be easier for you to remember.

Indirect object pronouns: 3rd person

Singular		*Plural*	
le	*(to) you* (formal)/*him/her/it*	les	*(to) you* (formal)/*them*

Le and **les** become **se** before **lo, la, los, las.** *Se lo* daré, *I'll give it to you* (formal)/*him/her/it.*

Position of object pronouns

a Object pronouns normally precede the verb, *¿Me trae* un café?
b In sentences with two object pronouns, the indirect one comes first, **Te las daré,** *I'll give them to you.*
c With imperatives, they follow positive forms but come before negative ones, e.g. **Dígale, No le diga.**
d In constructions with a main verb followed by an infinitive (e.g. **llevar**) or a gerund (e.g. **haciendo**), the object pronoun can either precede the main verb or be attached to the infinitive or gerund, e.g. **Voy a llevarlo** or **Lo voy a llevar,** *I'm going to take it*; **Estoy escribiéndola** or **La estoy escribiendo,** *I'm writing it.*

Pronouns with prepositions

With prepositions, use **mí, ti,** for the first and second person singular, and subject pronouns, **él, ella, usted,** etc., for the remaining persons.

Para mí un café.	*Coffee for me.*
No iré sin ti.	*I won't go without you* (familiar).
Lo hice por él/ella.	*I did it for him/her.*

Note the special use of the preposition **con** in:

conmigo	*with me*
contigo	*with you* (familiar)

But note: **con él/ella/usted.**

Reflexive pronouns

These are **me, te, se, nos, os** and **se.** And they accompany reflexive verbs such as **levantarse,** e.g. **me levanto,** *I get up.*

Relative pronouns
Que who, that, which

Que is the most common relative pronoun and it is used to refer to people or things.

El chico *que* **está allí** **es mi amigo.**	*The boy who's there is my friend.*
El tren *que* **va a Madrid** **es ése.**	*The train that/which is going to Madrid is that one.*

Quien, quienes who

Quien can only be used for people and it is used after a preposition.

La persona con *quien* me viste es mi hermana.	*The person with whom you saw me is my sister.*

El que

El (or la, los, las) que can refer to people or things and, like quien, it is used after a preposition.

Ése es *el* señor con *el que* debes hablar.	*That's the gentleman you must speak with.*
La empresa para *la que* trabajábamos cerró.	*The company we worked for closed down.*

Lo que what

No sé *lo que* pasa.	*I don't know what happens.*

Cuyo/a, cuyos/as whose

Andrés Pérez, *cuya* boda tuvo lugar ayer, es famoso.	*Andrés Pérez, whose wedding took place yesterday, is famous.*

6 Demonstratives

	masculine	feminine	
singular	este	esta	*this, this one*
plural	estos	estas	*these, these ones*
singular	ese	esa	*that, that one*
plural	esos	esas	*those, those ones*
singular	aquel	aquella	*that, that one*
plural	aquellos	aquellas	*those, those ones*

Neuter forms are: **esto**, *this*; **eso**, *that*; **aquello**, *that*, e.g. ¿Qué es esto/eso? *What's this/that?*

Aquel, aquella, etc., are used to refer to something or someone that is far from you.

When demonstratives are used as pronouns, meaning *this one*, *that one*, etc., they are normally written with an accent, for example Me gusta éste, *I like this one.*

7 Possessives

Short forms

	Singular	*Plural*	
	mi	mis	*my*
	tu	tus	*your* (familiar)
	su	sus	*your* (formal)
			his, her, its
masc/fem.	nuestro/a	nuestros/as	*our*
masc./fem.	vuestro/a	vuestros/as	*your* (familiar)
	su	sus	*your* (formal)
			their

The short form of possessives function as adjectives and they agree with the noun referred to, not with the owner, e.g. **nuestra casa**, *our house*; **nuestros amigos**, *our friends*.

Long forms

	Singular	*Plural*	
masc/fem.	mío/a	míos/as	*mine*
masc/fem.	tuyo/a	tuyos/as	*yours* (familiar)
masc/fem.	suyo/a	suyos/as	*yours* (formal)
			his, hers, its
masc/fem.	nuestro/a	nuestros/as	*ours*
masc./fem.	vuestro/a	vuestros/as	*yours* (familiar)
masc./fem.	suyo/a	suyos/as	*yours* (formal)
			theirs

Like the short forms, the long forms agree with the thing possessed, not with the owner, e.g. **un pariente mío**, *a relative of mine*; **Esas cartas son tuyas**, *Those letters are yours*.

Note that Latin Americans do not use the **vuestro** form of possessives, which is replaced by the phrase **de ustedes** or the possessive **suyo**, e.g. **Este apartamento es de ustedes/suyo, ¿verdad?**, *This apartment is yours, isn't it?*

8 Prepositions

Only the most common prepositions and meanings are given here.

a

at: *a* las 4.00, *at 4.00*
on: *a* la derecha/izquierda, *on the right/left*
a: una vez *a* la semana, *once a week*
personal a: used before the direct object when this is a person:
       Invité *a* Manuel, *I invited Manuel.*

con

| with: | café *con* leche | coffee with milk |

de

from:	Julio es *de* Granada.	Julio is from Granada.
made of:	*de* lana	woollen
in:	la ciudad más grande de México	the biggest city in Mexico

desde

| from: | *desde* las 2.00 de la tarde | from 2.00 in the afternoon |
| for: | *desde* hace cinco años | for five years |

en

in:	viven *en* Salamanca	they live in Salamanca
on:	las llaves están *en* la cama	the keys are on the bed
at:	trabaja *en* la Universidad de Madrid	he works at Madrid university

hasta

| until: | *hasta* las 5.00 | until 5.00 |
| as far as: | *hasta* el semáforo | as far as the traffic lights |

Para and por

Para and por tend to be confused by English speakers, as both can translate into English as *for*. Special treatment has been given to them here, with their main uses and meanings clearly defined.

para

length of time (for):

| Quiero una habitación *para* dos noches. | I want a room for two nights. |

with time phrases (for, by):

| Lo necesito *para* el jueves. | I need it for/by Thursday. |

direction (for):

| Salió *para* Barcelona. | He/she left for Barcelona. |

purpose (so, in order to):

| Te prestaré el libro *para* que lo leas. | I'll lend you the book so that you can read it. |
| Llamaré *para* confirmar | I'll call to (in order to) confirm. |

before names and personal pronouns (for):

| *Para* Ana es muy difícil. | For Ana it's very difficult. |
| *Para* mí un té con limón. | Lemon tea for me. |

with words such as muy, suficiente, bastante, demasiado *(to)*:

No hay bastante dinero *para* comprarlo.	*There isn't enough money to buy it.*
Es demasiado tarde *para* decírselo.	*It's too late to tell him/her.*

por

in time phrases (in, at):

Él saldrá *por* la mañana.	*He'll leave in the morning.*
Llegaremos *por* la noche.	*We'll arrive at night.*

means (by, over, through):

Viajarán *por* avión.	*They'll travel by plane.*
Me lo dijeron *por* teléfono.	*They told me over the phone.*
Lo supe *por* Carmen.	*I found out through Carmen.*

movement (through, along):

Pasaremos *por* Madrid.	*We'll go through Madrid.*
Continúe *por* esta calle.	*Continue along this street.*

cost, measure and number (for, a, per):

Pagué dos mil euros *por* él.	*I paid two thousand euros for it.*
Cobran trescientos *por* hora.	*They charge three hundred an/per hour.*
Subió un 10 *por* cien/ciento.	*It went up 10 per cent.*
Viajan a España tres veces *por/al* año.	*They travel to Spain three times a/per year.*

reason or cause (for, because of):

Lo hice *por* ti.	*I did it for you.*

purpose or aim (for)

Lo hizo *por* el dinero.	*He/she did it for the money.*
Fue *por/a por* (*Spain*) pan.	*He/she went for/to get some bread.*

indicating proximity (around, nearby):

¿Hay un hotel *por* aquí?	*Is there a hotel around here/ nearby?*

introducing the agent in passive sentences with ser (by):

Fue hecho *por* ella.	*It was made by her.*

9 Verbs

Types of verb

(a) -ar, -er, -ir

According to the ending of the infinitive, Spanish verbs may be grouped into three main categories: -ar, -er and -ir, e.g. **hablar**, *to speak*; **comer**, *to eat*; **vivir**, *to live*.

(b) Regular and irregular verbs

Most Spanish verbs are regular, that is, they follow a fixed pattern in their conjugation, but some very common verbs are irregular. A list of these can be found on pages 203–6.

(c) Stem-changing verbs

There are certain verbs which undergo a change in the stem, for example -e into -ie or -o into -ue when the vowel within the stem or root is stressed, for example **querer**, **quiero** *I want*, **poder**, **puedo** *I can*. (See paragraph 3, Unit 8.)

(d) Reflexive verbs

Verbs like **levantarse**, *to get up*, **acostarse**, *to go to bed*, **lavarse**, *to wash*, which carry the particle **se** attached to them are called reflexive. These are used with reflexive pronouns, for example **me levanto**, *I get up*. Reflexive verbs, if they are regular, are conjugated in the normal way. (See Reflexive pronouns above, and paragraph 1, Unit 9.)

10 The indicative tenses

The formation of each of the tenses is shown below through three regular verbs, representing each of the three conjugations: **hablar**, *to speak*, **comer**, *to eat*, **vivir**, *to live*. Only the present tense is given here in full with the corresponding subject pronouns. For irregular verbs look up pages 203–6.

Present indicative tense

Formation

yo	hablo	como	vivo
tú	hablas	comes	vives
Vd./él/ella	habla	come	vive
nosotros/as	hablamos	comemos	vivimos
vosotros/as	habláis	coméis	vivís
Vds./ellos/ellas	hablan	comen	viven

For irregular verbs in the present see pages 56–7.

Uses

a To refer to an action taking place at the moment of speaking.

¿Qué haces? *What are you doing?*

b To refer to habitual actions.

Me levanto a las 8.00. *I get up at 8.00.*

c To refer to something which is generally true.

En Brasil se habla *In Brazil they speak*
portugués. *Portuguese.*

d To refer to future actions, especially with verbs of movement.

Salimos mañana a las 3.00. *We leave tomorrow at 3.00.*

e To give directions and instructions.

Sigues por esta calle hasta *You go along this street*
el semáforo. *as far as the traffic light.*
Subes a la tercera planta *You go up to the third floor*
y me esperas allí. *and wait for me there.*

f To refer to the past, in a historical context.

En 1939 termina la guerra. *The war ends in 1939.*

Preterite tense
Formation

Verbs in **-er** and **-ir** share the same endings.

$$habl-\begin{cases} \text{é} \\ \text{aste} \\ \text{ó} \\ \text{amos} \\ \text{asteis} \\ \text{aron} \end{cases} \qquad com-/viv-\begin{cases} \text{í} \\ \text{iste} \\ \text{ió} \\ \text{imos} \\ \text{isteis} \\ \text{ieron} \end{cases}$$

For irregular preterite forms see pages 123–4.

Uses

The preterite tense is used to refer to actions or events that were completed at a specific point in the past or which lasted over a definite period and ended in the past.

Ayer hablé con él. *I spoke to him yesterday.*

Imperfect tense
Formation

Verbs in -er and -ir share the same endings.

$$habl- \begin{cases} aba \\ abas \\ aba \\ ábamos \\ abais \\ aban \end{cases} \qquad com\text{-}/viv\text{-} \begin{cases} ía \\ ías \\ ía \\ íamos \\ íais \\ ían \end{cases}$$

For irregular imperfect forms see pages 133–4.

Uses

a Generally, to talk about actions whose beginning or end are not specified.

En aquel tiempo vivía conmigo.	*At that time he/she lived/was living with me.*

b To describe people, places and things known in the past.

La casa tenía dos dormitorios.	*The house had two bedrooms.*

c To say what people used to do.

Trabajaban en Buenos Aires.	*They used to work in Buenos Aires.*

d To refer to an action that was taking place when something else happened.

Cuando salíamos empezó a llover.	*When we were going out it started to rain.*

Future tense
Formation

The same endings, added to the whole infinitive, apply to -ar, -er and -ir verbs.

$$hablar\text{-}/comer\text{-}/vivir\text{-} \begin{cases} é \\ ás \\ á \\ emos \\ éis \\ án \end{cases}$$

For irregular verbs in the future see pages 105–6.

Uses

a To refer to a future action.

Mañana hablaré con él. *Tomorrow I'll speak to him.*

b To indicate probability and uncertainty.

Supongo que vivirá aquí. *I suppose he/she lives here.*
¿Qué hora será? *I wonder what time it is.*

c To express promises.

Prometo que te lo daré. *I promise I'll give it to you.*

d To give commands.

Te lo comerás todo. *You'll eat it all.*

Conditional tense
Formation

The same endings, added to the whole infinitive, apply to -**ar**, -**er** and -**ir** verbs.

$$\text{hablar-/comer-/vivir-} \begin{cases} \text{ía} \\ \text{ías} \\ \text{ía} \\ \text{íamos} \\ \text{íais} \\ \text{ían} \end{cases}$$

For irregular conditional forms see page 162.

Uses

a To say what you would do or would like to do.

Yo hablaría con ella. *I would speak to her.*
Nos gustaría ir. *We'd like to go.*

b As a sign of politeness in requests.

¿Sería tan amable de *Would you be kind enough*
venir aquí? *to come here?*

c In conditional sentences.

Si tuviera dinero lo *If I had money I would buy it.*
compraría.

Perfect tense
Formation

The perfect tense is formed with the present tense of **haber** followed by a past participle. This ends in -**ado** for -**ar** verbs and -**ido** for -**er** and -**ir** verbs.

| he
has
ha
hemos
habéis
han | habl*ado*
com*ido*
viv*ido* |

For irregular past participles see page 78.

Uses

a To talk about past events which relate to the present.

Ya has comido demasiado. *You've already eaten too much.*

b To talk about recent events.

Hoy he hablado con Pepe. *Today I have spoken with Pepe.*

c To refer to actions which have taken place over a period of time which has not yet ended.

Hemos vivido aquí largo tiempo. *We've lived here a long time.*

Note that, unlike the preterite, the perfect tense is not normally used when talking about actions which occurred at some specific point in the past such as *I spoke to her last week.*

Pluperfect tense
Formation

The pluperfect tense is formed with the imperfect of **haber** and a past participle.

| había
habías
había
habíamos
habíais
habían | habl*ado*
com*ido*
viv*ido* |

Use

The pluperfect tense is used for referring to actions which took place before some other past event.

La fiesta había terminado cuando llegué. *The party had finished when I arrived.*

Future perfect
Formation

The future perfect is formed with the future of **haber** followed by the past participle.

habré
habrás
habrá
habremos
habréis
habrán
} habl*ado*
com*ido*
viv*ido*

Uses

a To express probability.

¿Habrá llegado el tren?　*Do you think the train will have arrived?*

b To say that something will happen before a moment in the future.

Para las tres ya lo habré terminado.　*By three o'clock I will have finished it.*

Conditional perfect
Formation

The conditional perfect is formed with the conditional form of **haber** followed by a past participle.

habría
habrías
habría
habríamos
habríais
habrían
} habl*ado*
com*ido*
viv*ido*

Uses

a Generally, the conditional perfect is used for saying what one would have done.

Yo habría ido.　*I would have gone.*

b It is also found in sentences expressing unfulfilled conditions.

Si hubiera sabido, la habría llamado.　*If I had known, I would have called her.*

11 The subjunctive tenses

Uses of the subjunctive

The subjunctive is not normally used on its own but is dependent on another verb or phrase. Verbs which express hope, doubt, emotions, preferences and orders are among those requiring the use of the subjunctive in a subordinate clause introduced by **que**. The subject of the main clause must be different from that of the subordinate clause. (For more information on the use of the subjunctive see Units 21–23.)

Present subjunctive
Formation

To form the present subjunctive, remove the **-o** of the first person of the present tense indicative and add the endings, one set for **-ar** verbs, another for verbs ending in **-er** and **-ir**. This rule applies also to stem-changing verbs and most irregular verbs.

$$habl\text{-} \left\{ \begin{array}{l} e \\ es \\ e \\ emos \\ éis \\ en \end{array} \right. \qquad com\text{-/}viv\text{-} \left\{ \begin{array}{l} a \\ as \\ a \\ amos \\ áis \\ an \end{array} \right.$$

For irregular forms in the present subjunctive see pages 151–2.

Uses

The present subjunctive normally occurs in sentences which carry a main clause with a verb in the present indicative, but also sometimes in the future, the perfect or the imperative. Its uses are generally no different from those of the subjunctive as a whole, as you will see from the examples below. Only main uses are given here.

hope

Espero que regreses pronto. *I hope you come back soon.*

doubt

No creo que hablen español. *I don't think they speak Spanish.*

emotions

Siento que no puedas venir.	*I'm sorry you can't come.*
Me alegro de que les escribas.	*I'm glad you're writing to them.*

wishes and preferences

Quiero que me ayudes.	*I want you to help me.*
Prefiero que te lo comas tú.	*I'd rather you eat it.*

requirements with regard to someone or something

Buscan a alguien que hable español.	*They're looking for someone who speaks Spanish.*

possibility

Es posible que lleguen hoy.	*It's possible that they may arrive today.*

indirect commands

Les he dicho que me llamen.	*I've told them to call me.*
Le pediré que lo compre.	*I'll ask him/her to buy it.*
Dile que lo venda.	*Tell him/her to sell it.*

with expressions such as cuando, hasta que, *when they refer to the future*

Comeremos cuando llegues.	*We'll eat when you arrive.*

with the phrase para que, *which indicates purpose*

He traído la carta para que la leas.	*I've brought the letter so that you can read it.*

Imperfect subjunctive
Formation

There are two alternative endings for the imperfect subjunctive, which are generally interchangeable. The first, which seems to be more common, is directly derived from the third person plural of the preterite.

Preterite (3rd person pl.)		*Imperfect subjunctive* (1st and 3rd person sing.)
hablaron	*they spoke*	**hablara**
comieron	*they ate*	**comiera**
vivieron	*they lived*	**viviera**

Here are the full forms for the two alternative endings:

$$habl- \begin{cases} \text{ara/ase} \\ \text{aras/ases} \\ \text{ara/ase} \\ \text{áramos/ásemos} \\ \text{arais/aseis} \\ \text{aran/asen} \end{cases} \qquad com\text{-}/viv\text{-} \begin{cases} \text{iera/iese} \\ \text{ieras/ieses} \\ \text{iera/iese} \\ \text{iéramos/iésemos} \\ \text{ierais/ieseis} \\ \text{ieran/iesen} \end{cases}$$

For irregular imperfect subjunctive forms see page 159.

Uses

The imperfect subjunctive occurs in sentences which carry a main clause with a verb in the past or conditional. Its uses are generally those of the subjunctive as a whole, but it also occurs in conditional sentences expressing ideas such as *if they called me...*, *if they spoke Spanish...* . Here are some examples:

Yo esperaba que me ayudaras (or **ayudases**).	*I was hoping you would help me.*
Él no quiso que lo comprara (or **comprase**).	*He didn't want me to buy it.*
Nos pidió que esperáramos (or **esperásemos**).	*He/she asked us to wait.*
Me gustaría que volvieran (or **volviesen**).	*I'd like them to come back.*
Si me llamaran (or **llamasen**) **los invitaría.**	*If they called me I'd invite them.*

Perfect subjunctive
Formation

The perfect subjunctive is formed with the present subjunctive of **haber** followed by a past participle.

$$\left.\begin{matrix} \text{haya} \\ \text{hayas} \\ \text{haya} \\ \text{hayamos} \\ \text{hayáis} \\ \text{hayan} \end{matrix}\right\} \quad \begin{matrix} \text{hablado} \\ \text{comido} \\ \text{vivido} \end{matrix}$$

Uses

The uses of this tense correspond to those of the subjunctive as a whole. It usually occurs in subordinate clauses with the verb in the main clause in the present tense indicative.

No creo que Luis haya llegado.	*I don't think Luis has arrived.*

Espero que me hayas entendido.	*I hope you have understood me.*	**197** grammar reference

Pluperfect subjunctive
Formation

This is formed with the imperfect subjunctive of **haber,** with its two alternative endings **-ra** or **-se,** followed by a past participle.

hubiera/hubiese hubieras/hubieses hubiera/hubiese hubiéramos/hubiésemos hubierais/hubieseis hubieran/hubiesen	habl*ado* com*ido* viv*ido*

Uses

This tense is normally associated with the expression of unfulfilled conditions.

Si hubiera (or **hubiese**) **llovido no habríamos ido.**	*If it had rained we wouldn't have gone.*
Si hubieras (or **hubieses**) **estudiado habrías aprobado.**	*If you had studied you would have passed.*

The **-ra** form of the pluperfect subjunctive is often used in place of the conditional perfect.

Si lo hubiera (or **hubiese**) **sabido no hubiera** (or **habría**) **venido.**	*If I had known I wouldn't have come.*

12 Imperative
Formation

Spanish uses different imperative forms depending on who you are talking to (familiar or formal) and whether you are speaking to one or more than one person (singular or plural). Familiar imperatives have different positive and negative forms.

To form the imperative for **usted,** change the ending of the 3rd person singular of the present tense indicative from **-a** to **-e** for **-ar** verbs, and from **-e** to **-a** for verbs ending in **-er** and **-ir.** For the plural add an **-n.**

present tense	*usted*	*ustedes*
Vd. habl*a*	habl*e*	habl*en*
Vd. com*e*	com*a*	com*an*
Vd. viv*e*	viv*a*	viv*an*

To form the imperative for **tú**, remove the -s from the second person singular of the present tense. For **vosotros**, remove the **-r** of the infinitive and replace it by a **-d**.

infinitive	*present tense*	*tú*	*vosotros*
habl*ar*	tú habl*as*	habla	habla*d*
com*er*	tú com*es*	come	com*ed*
viv*ir*	tú viv*es*	vive	viv*id*

Negative imperatives are formed with the present subjunctive. All you need to do is put **no** before the corresponding verb form.

usted	*ustedes*	*tú*	*vosotros*
no habl*e*	no habl*en*	no habl*es*	no habl*éis*
no com*a*	no com*an*	no com*as*	no com*áis*
no viv*a*	no viv*an*	no viv*as*	no viv*áis*

For irregular imperatives see pages 141 and 143.

Uses

The imperative is used in instructions, directions and commands.

Lea las instrucciones cuidadosamente.	*Read the instructions carefully.*
Gire a la derecha en la esquina.	*Turn right at the corner.*
No hables con él.	*Don't speak to him.*

Pronouns with imperatives

Object and reflexive pronouns are attached to the ending of positive imperatives. With negative imperatives they precede the verb.

¡Déjame solo!	*Leave me alone!*
¡No me dejes solo!	*Don't leave me alone!*
Siéntese allí.	*Sit down there.*
No se siente allí.	*Don't sit there.*

13 Government of verbs

Main verb + infinitive

As in English, the construction main verb + infinitive is very common in Spanish, as you will see from the examples below.

a With verbs denoting wants and likes, e.g. **querer** *to want*, **preferir** *to prefer*, **gustar** *to like*.

Quieren volver.	*They want to come back.*
Me gusta bailar.	*I like to dance.*

b With verbs denoting ability and capacity, e.g. **poder** *to be able to, can*, **saber** *to know how to.*

| No puedo hacerlo. | *I can't do it.* |
| No sé nadar. | *I don't know how to swim.* |

c With verbs of perception, e.g. **ver** *to see*, **oír** *to hear.*

| La vimos salir. | *We saw her go out.* |
| No la oí entrar. | *I didn't hear her come in.* |

d Certain verbs are always used with an infinitive, for example **acabar de** *to have just*, **acostumbrar** *to be in the habit of*, **deber** *must, have to*, **dejar de** *to give up, to stop doing something*, **empezar** *to begin*, **soler** *to be in the habit of.*

Acaba de llegar.	*He/she has just arrived.*
No acostumbro hacer eso.	*I'm not in the habit of doing that.*
Debemos esperar.	*We must wait.*
Dejó de fumar.	*He/she gave up smoking.*
Empezó a llover.	*It started to rain.*
No suelen venir aquí.	*They don't usually come here.*

Main verb + gerund

The gerund is that form of the verb which in English ends in -*ing*, e.g. *working*. In Spanish this is formed by adding **-ando** to the stem of **-ar** verbs and **-iendo** to that of **-er** and **-ir** verbs. There are a number of constructions with the gerund in Spanish, of which the most common are the following:

a With **estar**, to indicate an action in progress.

| Están trabajando. | *They're working.* |

b With **llevar** followed by a time expression to denote *for.*

| Llevamos un año viviendo aquí. | *We've been living here for a year.* |

c With **seguir** and **continuar** *to continue, go on.*

| Sigue viviendo allí. | *He/she continues living there.* |
| Continuaremos andando. | *We'll continue walking.* |

Main verb + past participle

The past participle is formed by adding **-ado** to the stem of **-ar** verbs and **-ido** to that of verbs ending in **-er** and **-ir**. The two most important constructions with the past participle are the following:

a With **haber**, auxiliary verb *to have*, to form compound tenses.

| Hemos terminado. | *We have finished.* |
| Se han ido. | *They've left.* |

b With **estar**, to denote a state which is the result of an action. Here the past participle agrees in gender and number with the noun it refers to.

La habitación está reservada. *The room is booked.*
Los museos están cerrados. *The museums are closed.*

14 Using *se*

Se is used with the third person of the verb.

a To form impersonal sentences, e.g. ¿Cómo se va al aeropuerto desde aquí?

b To convey the idea that something *'is done'*, e.g. **Aquí se habla español.**

c With reflexive verbs (e.g. **levantarse**), e.g. **Se levantaron a las 6.00.**

15 Using *ser* and *estar*

Ser is used

a To give personal information such as who you are, nationality, where you are from, occupation, marital status (L.Am.), e.g. **Plácido Domingo es español**, *Plácido Domingo is Spanish.*

b To describe people, places and things, e.g. **Barcelona es una ciudad preciosa**, *Barcelona is a very beautiful city.*

c With the time and certain time phrases, e.g. **Mañana es domingo**, *Tomorrow is Sunday.*

d To refer to the material something is made of, e.g. **Esta camisa es de algodón**, *This shirt is made of cotton.*

e To denote possession, e.g. **Este libro es mío**, *This book is mine.*

f To ask and say how much something is, e.g. ¿Cuánto es?, *How much is it?*

g To indicate where an event will take place, e.g. **La fiesta es en casa de Isabel**, *The party is in Isabel's house.*

h To denote characteristics which are considered universal or part of someone's nature, e.g. **La Tierra es redonda**, *The Earth is round.*

i In passive constructions followed by a past participle, e.g. **El cuadro fue robado**, *The picture was stolen.*

j With a noun complement, e.g. **Es un ordenador/ computador/una computadora (L.Am.)**, *It's a computer.*

Estar is used

a To ask and say where something is, e.g. **La catedral está en la plaza**, *The cathedral is in the square.*

b To express marital status, e.g. **Paco está soltero**, *Paco is single.*

c To ask people how they are and respond, e.g. **¿Cómo estás? Estoy bien**, *How are you?, I'm well.*

d To denote a temporary state or condition, e.g. **Gloria está muy guapa hoy**, *Gloria is looking very pretty today.*

e To refer to cost when prices fluctuate, e.g. **¿A cuánto está (el cambio de) la libra?**, *How much is (What's the rate of exchange for) the pound?*

f With past participles, to denote a condition resulting from an action, e.g. **El restaurante está abierto**, *The restaurant is open.*

g With gerunds, to talk about actions in progress, e.g. **Está bañándose**, *He/she is having a bath.*

16 Stress, accentuation and spelling

Stress and accentuation

a Words which end in a vowel, **n** or **s** stress the last syllable but one, e.g. **na**da, **to**man, **hi**jos.

b Words which end in a consonant other than **n** or **s** stress the last syllable, e.g. **Ma**d**rid**, **espa**ño**l**.

c Words which do not follow the above rules carry a written accent over the vowel of the stressed syllable, e.g. **allí**, **autobús**, **invitación**.

d Differences in meaning between words which are spelt in the same way are shown through the use of an accent:

sí	*yes*	si	*if*
él	*he*	el	*the* (masc.)
sé	*I know*	se	*pronoun*
mí	*me*	mi	*my*
dé	*give*	de	*of, from*

e Question words carry an accent, e.g. **¿dónde?**, **¿cuándo?**

Spelling

Note the following changes in spelling.

a Nouns and adjectives which end in z change the z into c to form the plural, e.g. **el lápiz** *pencil*, **los lápices** *pencils*.

b Some verbs may change the spelling in certain forms in order to keep the same sound of the infinitive, e.g. **llegar** *to arrive*, **llegué** *I arrived*; **coger** *to take, catch*, **cojo** *I take, catch*; **sacar** *to take out*, **saqué** *I took out*.

c A spelling change may also occur because of an accent in the infinitive or because there would otherwise be more than two vowels together, e.g. **caer** *to fall*, **cayó** *he/she/it fell*, **cayeron** *you/they fell*; **leer** *to read*, **leyó** *he/she read*, **leyeron** *you/they read*; **oír** *to hear*, **oyó** *he/she/it heard*, **oyeron** *you/they heard*.

17 Numbers

Cardinal numbers

a Cardinal numbers, for example **dos**, **cuatro**, **veinte**, **cuarenta**, are adjectives but they are invariable, except for forms involving **un(o)/-a** and **cientos/-as**, which agree in gender with the following noun, e.g. **una** libra *one pound*; **doscientos** invitados *two hundred guests*.

b **Ciento** is shortened to **cien** before a noun or an adjective, e.g. **cien** dólares *one hundred dollars*.

c **Cien** and **mil** are not preceded by the indefinite article, e.g. **cien** kilómetros *a hundred kilometres*.

d **un millón** is preceded by the indefinite article and followed by **de**, e.g. Tengo **un millón de** cosas que hacer *I have a million things to do*.

Ordinal numbers

a Ordinal numbers agree in number and gender with the noun they refer to, e.g. el **segundo** día *the second day*; las **primeras** acciones *the first actions*.

b **Primero** and **tercero** drop the final -o before a masculine singular noun, e.g. el **tercer** autobús *the third bus*.

The following list includes only the most common irregular verbs. Only irregular forms are given (verbs marked with an asterisk are also radical-changing).

abrir *to open*
past particple: abierto

andar *to walk*
preterite: anduve, anduviste, anduvo, anduvimos, anduvisteis, anduvieron

conducir *to drive*
present indicative: (yo) conduzco
present subjunctive: conduzca, conduzcas, conduzca, conduzcamos, conduzcáis, conduzcan
preterite: conduje, condujiste, condujo, condujimos, condujisteis, condujeron

dar *to give*
present indicative: (yo) doy
preterite: di, diste, dio, dimos, disteis, dieron
present subjunctive: dé, des, dé, demos, deis, den

decir* *to say*
present indicative: (yo) digo
present subjunctive: diga, digas, diga, digamos, digáis, digan
preterite: dije, dijiste, dijo, dijimos, dijisteis, dijeron
future: diré, dirás, dirá, diremos, diréis, dirán
conditional: diría, dirías, diría, diríamos, diríais, dirían
imperative (familiar, singular): di
gerund: diciendo
past participle: dicho

escribir *to write*
past participle: escrito

estar *to be*
present indicative: estoy, estás, está, estamos, estáis, están
present subjunctive: esté, estés, esté, estemos, estéis, estén
preterite: estuve, estuviste, estuvo, estuvimos, estuvisteis,
 estuvieron
imperative (familiar, singular): está

hacer *to do, make*
present indicative: (yo) hago
present subjunctive: haga, hagas, haga, hagamos, hagáis,
 hagan
preterite: hice, hiciste, hizo, hicimos, hicisteis, hicieron
future: haré, harás, hará, haremos, haréis, harán
conditional: haría, harías, haría, haríamos, haríais, harían
imperative: (Vd.) haga, (tú) haz
past participle: hecho

ir *to go*
present indicative: voy, vas, va, vamos, vais, van
present subjunctive: vaya, vayas, vaya, vayamos, vayáis, vayan
imperfect: iba, ibas, iba, íbamos, ibais, iban
preterite: fui, fuiste, fue, fuimos, fuisteis, fueron
imperative: (Vd.) vaya, (tú) ve

leer *to read*
preterite: (él, ella, Vd.) leyó, (ellos, ellas, Vds.) leyeron
gerund: leyendo

oír *to hear*
present indicative: oigo, oyes, oye, oímos, oís, oyen
present subjunctive: oiga, oigas, oiga, oigamos, oigáis, oigan
preterite: (él, ella, Vd.) oyó, (ellos, ellas, Vds.) oyeron
imperative: (Vd.) oiga, (tú) oye
gerund: oyendo

poder* *to be able to, can*
preterite: pude, pudiste, pudo, pudimos, pudisteis, pudieron
future: podré, podrás, podrá, podremos, podréis, podrán
conditional: podría, podrías, podría, podríamos, podríais,
 podrían

poner *to put*
present indicative: (yo) pongo
present subjunctive: ponga, pongas, ponga, pongamos,
 pongáis, pongan

preterite: puse, pusiste, puso, pusimos, pusisteis, pusieron
future: pondré, pondrás, pondrá, pondremos, pondréis,
   pondrán
conditional: pondría, pondrías, pondría, pondríamos,
   pondríais, pondrían
imperative: (Vd.) ponga, (tú) pon
past participle: puesto

querer* *to want*
preterite: quise, quisiste, quiso, quisimos, quisisteis, quisieron
future: querré, querrás, querrá, querremos, querréis, querrán
conditional: querría, querrías, querría, querríamos, querríais,
   querrían

saber *to know*
present indicative: (yo) sé
present subjunctive: sepa, sepas, sepa, sepamos, sepáis, sepan
preterite: supe, supiste, supo, supimos, supisteis, supieron
future: sabré, sabrás, sabrá, sabremos, sabréis, sabrán
conditional: sabría, sabrías, sabría, sabríamos, sabríais, sabrían
imperative: (Vd.) sepa

salir *to go out*
present indicative: (yo) salgo
present subjunctive: salga, salgas, salga, salgamos, salgáis,
   salgan
future: saldré, saldrás, saldrá, saldremos, saldréis, saldrán
conditional: saldría, saldrías, saldría, saldríamos, saldríais,
   saldrían
imperative: (Vd.) salga, (tú) sal

ser *to be*
present indicative: soy, eres, es, somos, sois, son
present subjunctive: sea, seas, sea, seamos, seáis, sean
preterite: fui, fuiste, fue, fuimos, fuisteis, fueron
imperfect indicative: era, eras, era, éramos, erais, eran
imperative: (Vd.) sea, (tú) sé

tener* *to have*
present indicative: (yo) tengo
present subjunctive: tenga, tengas, tenga, tengamos, tengáis,
   tengan
preterite: tuve, tuviste, tuvo, tuvimos, tuvisteis, tuvieron
future: tendré, tendrás, tendrá, tendremos, tendréis, tendrán
conditional: tendría, tendrías, tendría, tendríamos, tendríais,
   tendrían
imperative: (Vd.) tenga, (tú) ten

traer *to bring*
present indicative: (yo) traigo
present subjunctive: traiga, traigas, traiga, traigamos, traigáis, traigan
preterite: traje, trajiste, trajo, trajimos, trajisteis, trajeron
imperative: (Vd.) traiga
gerund: trayendo

venir* *to come*
present indicative: (yo) vengo
present subjunctive: venga, vengas, venga, vengamos, vengáis, vengan
preterite: vine, viniste, vino, vinimos, vinisteis, vinieron
future: vendré, vendrás, vendrá, vendremos, vendréis, vendrán
conditional: vendría, vendrías, vendría, vendríamos, vendríais, vendrían
imperative: (Vd.) venga, (tú) ven
gerund: viniendo

ver *to see*
present indicative: (yo) veo
present subjunctive: vea, veas, vea, veamos, veáis, vean
imperfect indicative: veía, veías, veía, veíamos, veíais, veían
imperative: (Vd.) vea
past participle: visto

volver* *to come back*
past participle: vuelto

taking it further

Further study

There are a number of books on sale which may help you to expand your present knowledge of Spanish grammar. The following recommended textbooks may help you to achieve that:

Butt, J., *Oxford Spanish Grammar*, Oxford University Press, 1996

Kattán-Ibarra, J. and Pountain, C. J., *Modern Spanish Grammar*, Routledge, 2nd edition, 2003

Muñoz, P. and Thacker, M., *A Spanish Learning Grammar*, Arnold, 2001

Turk, P. and Zollo, M., *¡Acción gramática!*, Hodder and Stoughton, 1993

Sources of authentic Spanish

Spanish newspapers

El País (http://www.elpais.es)
El Mundo (http://www.el-mundo.es)
La Vanguardia (http://www.lavanguardia.es)
ABC (http://www.abc.es)
El Periódico (http://www.elperiodico.es/).

Spanish magazines

For general information, including Spanish current affairs and world news, try the following:

Cambio 16   Tiempo   Tribuna   Época

For light reading and entertainment you might like to look at the following:

Hola   Quo   Mía
Lecturas   Pronto   Semana, etc.

These are by far the most popular amongst Spaniards and, as a beginner, you may find some of the articles easier to follow.

Latin American newspapers and magazines

Latin American newspapers and magazines will be more difficult to find outside each country, but if you have internet facilities you will be able to access their websites, although they may be special net versions.

Argentina
La Nación (http://lanacion.com.ar)
Clarín (http://www.clarin.com.ar)

Chile
El Mercurio (http://www.elmercurio.cl)

Colombia
El Espectador (http://www.elespectador.com)

Cuba
Granma (http://www.granma.cubaweb.cu)

Mexico
El Universal (http://www.el-universal.com.mx)

Peru
El Comercio (http://elcomercioperu.com.pe)
Correo (http://www.correoperu.com.pe)

Radio and television

An excellent way to improve your understanding of spoken Spanish is to listen to radio and watch television. On medium wave after dark and via satellite you will be able to gain access to Radio Nacional de España, Televisión Española (TVE) and other stations. And for spoken Latin American Spanish, you may like to tune in to the BBC Spanish Latin American Service, which can be heard on short wave.

Travelling in Spain and Latin America

Travelling in a Spanish-speaking country is probably the best way to practise what you have learnt and improve your command of the spoken language. If you are planning to do this, there are a number of good guidebooks which will help you to plan your journey. The well-known *Lonely Planet* series covers not just specific countries, but also the main regions and cities, including Spain and Latin America. For the latter, the *Mexico and Central American Handbook* and the *South American Handbook* have a long tradition amongst travellers in the region. *Time Out*, *Michelin* and *Fodor's*, among several others, have also become well established in the travelling market.

For travellers in Spain, the following websites may prove useful, with information on tourist attractions, accommodation, travel, restaurants, etc.:

Travelling to Spain: http://www.SiSpain.org/english/travelli/
Spain Today (local section of the *Europe Today* travel guide):
    http://www.wtg-online.com/data/esp/esp.asp
All about Spain: http://www.red2000.com/
Páginas amarillas del viajero (Yellow pages for travellers):
    http://www.spaindata.com/data/1index.shtm/

For the Spanish National Tourist Office try:

    http://www.tourspain.co.uk
    http://www.spaintour.com/offices.htm

Travellers in Latin America will find useful information in:

Travel Latin America: http://www.travellatinamerica.com/es/
Latin America – travel notes:
    http://www. travelnotes.org/LatinAmerica/index.htm
Travel Latin America: http://travellatinamerica.com

Culture and history

If you are interested in the culture and history of the Spanish-speaking countries, there are a number of publications in English which deal with such matters, some in less detail than others. Publications in Spanish usually require a much higher level of language than what you may have at present, but some are geared towards students of Hispanic studies and may be easier to follow. The best thing is to seek advice from a specialist bookseller of foreign-language books.

Internet users interested in Spain may like to try the following sites:

Historia – Sí Spain: http://www.sispain.org/spanish/history
About.com – Spanish culture:
    http://spanishculture.about.com/
Secretaría de Estado y Cultura de España (for a virtual visit to El Prado Museum): http://museoprado.mcu.es

Users searching for other information and websites on the Spanish net may find what they need in *Sí – Spain*:
    http://www.sispain.org/english/otherweb.html

For Latin America go to
Internet resources for Latin America:
    http://lib.nmsu.edu/subject/bord/index.html
Latin American Network Information Center:
    http://lanic.utexas.edu/las.html

Spanish language courses

The Instituto Cervantes, a worldwide organization, offers courses in Spanish and promotes Spanish culture in general; the Hispanic Council, in the United Kingdom, based in London, may be able to help you with enquiries about Spanish language courses and aspects of life in Spain. For information on Latin American Spanish you can contact the Hispanic Council or the embassy of the country you are interested in.

Information on Spanish language courses in Spain can also be found on a number of websites, several of which relate to specific language schools. For more general information and listings of schools you might like to look up:

Instituto Cervantes: http://www.cervantes.es/
Language schools – learning vacations:
    http://www.learningvacations.com

For Latin American Spanish, go to

Spanish language schools:
    http://www.ibw.com.ni/~nssmga/
Worldwide Classroom – Mexico schools:
    http://www.worldwide.edu/ci/mexico/index.htm/

key to the exercises

Unit 1

1 a Me llamo (name). **b** Soy (nationality). **c** Soy de (town or city). **d** Soy (occupation). **e** Estoy/soy (marital status). **2** ¿Cómo te llamas?/¿Eres español?/¿Eres de Buenos Aires?/¿Eres estudiante? **3 a** A. Morales es taxista. **b** S. Pérez es peluquera. **c** A. Muñoz es mecánico. **d** J. González es camarero/mesero. **e** J. Díaz es médico. **f** F. Mella es estudiante.

Unit 2

1 a quién. **b** cuál. **c** quiénes. **d** qué. **e** cuál. **f** cuáles. **2** ¿cómo estás?/presento/éste/gusto/ésta/éstos.

Unit 3

1 a Paco y Pepe son (muy) gordos. **b** Paloma es (muy) alta. **c** Javier está (muy) triste. **d** Rosa y Julio son/están (muy) elegantes. **e** El coche está (muy) limpio. **f** La Tierra es redonda. **2** Es una ciudad muy bonita. La gente es muy simpática y el clima es bastante bueno. No hace demasiado calor. El hotel es excelente. Tiene un restaurante muy bueno y dos bares. También tiene una playa estupenda. Estoy muy contento/a aquí.

Unit 4

1 a ¿Tiene restaurante el hotel? **b** ¿Hay piscina? **c** ¿Tiene una/alguna habitación doble? **d** ¿Tiene aparcamiento el hotel? **e** ¿Hay un/algún supermercado por aquí? **f** ¿Hay museos en la ciudad? **2** Follow example. **3** (1) es. (2) tiene. (3) es. (4) tiene/hay. (5) es. (6) hay. (7) hay. (8) tienen. (9) es. (10) tiene. (11) tiene. (12) es. (13) tiene/hay. (14) tiene.

Unit 5

1 a ¿Dónde está la catedral? **b** ¿Hay algún café por aquí? **c** ¿Dónde está el aparcamiento? **d** ¿Dónde está correos? **2** *Ejemplos* **a** Sí, hay dos. Uno está en la calle Mayor, entre el cine y el restaurante, y el otro está en la calle Miramar, en la esquina, al lado del hotel Sol. **b** Está a la derecha, enfrente del café. **c** Está a la izquierda, al final de la calle Mayor. **d** Está en la próxima calle a la izquierda, al lado del museo.

Unit 6

1 a mía. **b** de/de. **c** su. **d** mi/mis. **e** mías. **f** suya. **g** pertenece. **h** las. **2** (1) tu. (2) tu. (3) mía. (4) tus. (5) míos. (6) su. (7) tu. (8) su. (9) nuestro. (10) tuyo. **3 b** Ana y Luis no tienen tarjetas de crédito. **c** Yo (no) tengo ... **d** Juan no tiene una casa. **e** Ana y Luis tienen ... **f** Yo (no) tengo ... **g** Juan tiene coche/carro. **h** Ana y Luis tienen ... **i** Yo (no) tengo ...

Unit 7

1 a tenemos. **b** hay. **c** debes. **d** necesita. **e** hace falta. **f** necesario. **g** necesita. **h** imprescindible. **2 a** 5. **b** 4. **c** 6. **d** 3. **e** 1. **f** 2.

Unit 8

1 a juega/sé. **b** llueve/nieva. **c** entiende. **d** conozco/voy. **e** encuentro/recuerdo. **f** empieza/empezamos. **2 a** ¿Cuánto tiempo hace que vives en Madrid? Vivo en Madrid desde hace diez años. **b** ... trabajas .../Trabajo ... **c** ... estudias .../Estudio ... **d** ... conoces .../Conozco. **e** ... juegas .../Juego ... **f** ... haces .../Hago ... **3** 1–c. 2–f. 3–a. 4–e. 5–b. 6–d.

Unit 9

1 (1) hago. (2) me levanto. (3) desayuno. (4) ayudo. (5) voy. (6) oigo. (7) veo. (8) juego. (9) leo. (10) salgo. (11) vuelvo. (12) escribo. (13) llamo. (14) me acuesto. **2 a** ¿A qué hora te levantas normalmente? **b** ¿A qué hora sales de la oficina? **c** ¿A qué hora tienes clase? **d** ¿Te acuestas tarde? **e** ¿Qué haces los fines de semana? **f** ¿Qué sueles hacer en tus vacaciones? **3 a** Se levanta ... **b** Se va al trabajo ... **c** ... habla por teléfono. **d** ... vuelve a casa. **e** ... prepara la cena. **f** ... suele ver la televisión.

Unit 10

1 a ¿Puedes entender mi español? **b** ¿Puedes hablar más despacio? **c** ¿Puedes repetir, por favor? **d** ¿Sabes jugar al tenis? **e** Hoy no puedo jugar. Podemos jugar mañana. **f** No sé conducir. ¿Sabes conducir? **2** podemos/se puede/pueden/puede/ pueden/ puedo. **3 a** No se puede fumar. **b** No aparcar. **c** No se puede nadar. **d** No entrar. **e** No se puede girar/doblar a la izquierda. **f** No hacer/tomar fotografías.

Unit 11

1 Estudian ... realizan ... invitan ... hacen ... seleccionan ... llaman ... escogen. **2 a** se corta ... se fríe ... se le pone. **b** se selecciona ... se lleva ... se envía. **c** se eligen ... se evalúan.

Unit 12

1 Quisiéramos una habitación doble. ¿Tiene alguna?/Preferimos una exterior, pero quisiéramos verla. ¿Es posible?/Está bien, queremos tomar la habitación, pero quisiéramos saber cuánto cuesta./Queremos la habitación solamente. Preferimos comer fuera. **2** a–2. b–4. c–1. d–3. **3** 1–c. 2–a. 3–b. 4–d.

Unit 13

1 a le. **b** nos. **c** les. **d** mí. **e** ti. **f** le. **g** os. **h** nos. **2 a** ¿Te gusta la habitación? **b** ¿Te gusta cocinar? **c** ¿Qué música te gusta? **d** ¿Qué programas de televisión te gustan? **e** ¿Te gustan los animales? **f** ¿Qué te gusta hacer los fines de semana? **3** 1–c: A Rafael y su novia les gusta .... 2–f: A Juan le gusta .... 3–a: A Andrés le gusta .... 4–d: A Ángeles le gusta .... 5–b: A Paco le gusta .... 6–f: A María y su familia les gusta ...

Unit 14

1 a ¿Qué te parece la ciudad? **b** ¿Qué te parecen los museos? **c** ¿Qué opinas de los parques? **d** ¿Qué piensas de la gente? **e** ¿Qué opinas de mis amigos? **f** ¿Qué piensas de la vida en la ciudad? **2** (1) parece. (2) creo. (3) en mi opinión. (4) considero. (5) a mi parecer. (6) pienso. **3** El hotel es muy bueno, pero creo que la gente es un poco ruidosa/La playa me parece excelente/Sí, estoy libre. ¿Qué te parece si vamos a una disco?

Unit 15

1 a ¿Qué vas a hacer este verano? ¿Qué van a hacer . . .? **b** Voy a hacer un curso de inglés en Inglaterra. Vamos a viajar a la India. **c** Miguel va a hacer un curso de inglés en Inglaterra. María y Alberto van a viajar a la India. **d** Voy a (*your plans*). **2** (1) será. (2) saldré. (3) llegaré. (4) me quedaré. (5) llamaré. (6) podré. (7) tendré. (8) podremos. (9) vendrás. (10) tendrás. **3** 4–a, irá. 3–b, hará. 1–c, practicará. 2–d, estudiará.

Unit 16

1 a Por favor, ¿nos trae dos cafés? **b** . . . ¿me pasa . . .? **c** . . . ¿nos despierta . . .? **d** . . . ¿nos envía . . .? **e** . . . ¿nos da . . .? **f** . . . ¿me llama . . .? **2 a** ¿La ayudo? **b** ¿Le traigo una taza de café? **c** ¿La llevo a su hotel? **d** ¿La llamo mañana a las 9.00? **e** ¿Le enseño la ciudad? **f** ¿Le presento al gerente? **3** d

Unit 17

1 a–3, escribir. b–5, decir. c–1, romper. d–6, volver. e–7, hacer. f–2, abrir. g–4, poner. **2** Hola, soy (your name). ¿Está Ana?/Hola Ana, ¿estás libre esta noche?/¿Has visto la nueva película de Almodóvar? Me han dicho que es muy buena./He llamado al cine y me han dicho que hay una sesión a las 9.00. ¿Qué te parece?/De acuerdo. **3 b** hemos ido. **c** hemos alquilado. **d** he nadado. **e** hemos montado. **f** hemos hecho.

Unit 18

1 (1) volví. (2) pasé. (3) estuve. (4) gustó. (5) pareció. (6) fui. (7) conocimos. (8) invitaron. (9) fueron. (10) traje. **2 a** Sí, lo escribí anteayer. **b** Sí, las hice el lunes. **c** Sí, la llamé ayer por la mañana. **d** Sí, lo compré la semana pasada. **e** Sí, lo mandé anoche. **f** Sí, la respondí anteanoche/antenoche (L.Am.). **3 a** Carmen contestó el teléfono. **b** Pablo leyó la correspondencia. **c** Carmen envió faxes. **d** Pablo trabajó en el ordenador/la computadora (L. Am.). **e** Carmen atendió al público. **f** Pablo sirvió café a los clientes.

Unit 19

1 (1) se llamaba. (2) tenía. (3) era. (4) vestía. (5) era. (6) trabajaba. (7) compartía. (8) era. (9) tenía. (10) estudiaba. (11) tocaba. (12) gustaba. **2** (1) llegué. (2) tenía. (3) hacía. (4) había terminado. (5) sabía. (6) hice. (7) fue. (8) me quedé. (9) encontré. (10) era. (11) tenía. (12) ayudó. (13) ganaba. (14)

trabajé. **3** estaba en medio .../ tenía dos plantas/No era una casa .../pero era .../había un jardín/había una colina/había unos árboles/tenían un coche/tenía una bicicleta/tenía un perro/le gustaba.

Unit 20

1 Dialogue 1: sigue/gira/continúa. Dialogue 2: ven/ve/ingresa/ve/echa/pasa/tráeme/pregunta. **2 a** pongas/ponla. **b** dejes/llévalas. **c** traigas/déjalas. **d** cierres/cierra. **e** limpies/hazlo. **f** vayas/ve. **g** hagas/hazla. **h** tires/espera. **3** Example: Sigue todo recto por esta calle y en la esquina gira/dobla a la izquierda. En la segunda calle gira/dobla a la derecha. Sigue/continúa todo recto hasta la segunda calle y allí gira/dobla a la izquierda. La estación está al final de esa calle.

Unit 21

1 (1) hayas recibido. (2) vaya. (3) me quede. (4) estaré. (5) hayas conseguido. (6) estés. (7) pague. (8) encuentre. **2 a** Es una lástima que se divorcie. **b** Me alegro de que vuelva a España. **c** ¡Qué pena que no siga estudiando! **d** Me alegro de que vayan a comprar una casa. **e** Siento que esté enfermo. **f** Espero que vaya. **g** Me sorprende que lo deje. **h** ¡Qué lástima que se vayan! **3** 1–d. 2–c. 3–a. 4–b.

Unit 22

1 a vayamos. **b** nos quedáramos. **c** saliéramos. **d** invitáramos. **e** venga. **f** la hagas. **2** (1) informara. (2) llames. (3) recordara. (4) envíes. (5) pases. (6) lleves. **3** 1–c. 2–d. 3–b. 4–a. 5–f. 6–e.

Unit 23

1 a–4. b–5. c–1. d–6. e–3. f–2. **2** Querida Mari Carmen: Gracias por tu carta y tu invitación para visitarte en España. Desgraciadamente tengo que trabajar todo el verano, pero si estuviera libre por supuesto te visitaría. Me encantaría verte otra vez. Quizá para las Navidades si puedo, a menos que tú quieras venir y quedarte conmigo entonces. ¡Sería fantástico!

Me alegro de que hayas encontrado trabajo. Sé que no es lo que querías, pero es un trabajo. Yo también lo habría/hubiera tomado. Espero que te guste. **3** 1c: Si ganara la lotería construiría ... 2e: ... compraríamos/daríamos 3a: ... ... cambiaríamos 4f: ... iríamos/aprenderíamos 5b: ... haríamos/invitaríamos 6d: ... cambiaría/seguiría.

Spanish–English vocabulary

abajo *downstairs*
abogado/a *lawyer*
abuelos (m. pl.) *grandparents*
aburrido *boring*
acabar de *to have just*
aceptar *to accept*
acercarse *to approach, come near*
acompañar *to accompany*
acostarse *to go to bed*
acostumbrar *to be in the habit of*
acuerdo: de — *all right*
además *besides*
aeropuerto (m.) *airport*
agencia (f.) *agency*
agencia de viajes (f.) *travel agency*
ahora *now*
ahora mismo *right now*
alegrarse *to be glad*
algo *something, anything*
alguien *somebody, anybody*
alguna vez *ever*
alguno *some, any*
allí *there*
almorzar *to have lunch*
alquilar *to rent*
alquiler (m.) *rent*
alto *tall*
amable *kind*
amigo/a *friend*
andaluz *Andalusian*
antes *before*; lo — posible *as soon as possible*
año (m.) *year*
año pasado (m.) *last year*
Año Nuevo (m.) *New Year*
aparcamiento (m.) *car park*

aparcar *to park*
apartamento (m.) *apartment*
aprender *to learn*
aquí *here*
argentino *Argentinian*
arriba *upstairs*
arte (f.) *art*
artículo (m.) *article*
asistir *to attend*
asuntos exteriores (m. pl.) *foreign affairs*
atardecer (m.) *evening, dusk*
atender *to look after*
aunque *although*
auricular (m.) *receiver*
autoridad (f.) *authority*
avión (m.) *aeroplane*
ayer *yesterday*
ayudar *to help*
ayuntamiento (m.) *town hall*
azul *blue*

bailar *to dance*
bajar *to go down*
bajo *short*
banco (m.) *bank*
baño (m.) *bathroom*
barato *cheap*
barrio (m.) *district*
bastante *quite, enough*
beber *to drink*
biblioteca (f.) *library*
bicicleta (f.) *bicycle*
bien *well, good*
billete (m.) *ticket*
blanco *white*

blusa (f.) *blouse*
bolígrafo (m.) *ballpoint pen*
bolso (m.) *bag, handbag*
bonito *pretty*
botella (f.) *bottle*
británico *British*
bueno *good, well*
buenos días *good morning*
buscar *to fetch, come for, look for*

cabeza (f.) *head*
caer *to fall*
caja (f.) *case*
cajero automático (m.) *cash point*
caliente *hot*
calor (m.) *heat*; hace — *it's warm, hot*
caluroso *hot* (weather)
calle (f.) *street*
cama (f.) *bed*
camarero/a *waiter*
cambio (m.) *change*
camino (m.) *way*
camisa (f.) *shirt*
campesino/a *farmer*
campo (m.) *country, countryside*
carne (f.) *meat*
carnicería (f.) *butcher's*
caro *expensive*
carretera (f.) *highway, main road*
carta (f.) *letter, menu*
casa (f.) *house*
casado *married*
caso: en ese — *in that case*
catedral (f.) *cathedral*
católico *catholic*
cebolla (f.) *onion*
cena (f.) *dinner*
centro (m.) *centre*
centro deportivo (m.) *sports centre*
chaqueta (f.) *jacket*
chico (m.) *boy*
chileno *Chilean*
chuleta de cerdo (f.) *pork chop*
cine (m.) *cinema*
cita (f.) *appointment*
ciudad (f.) *city*
clima (m.) *climate*
cocina (f.) *kitchen*
cocinar *to cook*
coche (m.) *car*
coger *to take, catch*
colegio (m.) *school*
colombiano *Colombian*
color (m.) *colour*

comedor (m.) *dining room*
comer *to eat*
comida (f.) *food, lunch*
cómo *how*
cómodo *comfortable*
compartir *to share*
comprar *to buy*
comprimido (m.) *tablet*
conducir *to drive*
conmigo *with me*
conocer *to know, meet*
conseguir *to get*
considerar *to consider, think*
contaminado *polluted*
contar *to tell*
contar con *to have*
contigo *with you*
continuar *to continue*
contratar *to hire*
conversaciones (f. pl.) *talks*
copa (f.) *drink*
corbata (f.) *tie*
correos (m.) *post office*
correspondencia (f.) *mail*
cortar *to cut*
creer *to think*
cruzar *to cross*
cuál *which, what*
cuánto/s *how much/many*
cuarto de baño (m.) *bathroom*
cuenta (f.) *bill*
cuenta corriente (f.) *current account*
cumpleaños (m.) *birthday*
curso (m.) *course*

dar *to give*
datos personales (m. pl.) *personal information*
de *of, from*
deber *to have to, must*
deberes (m. pl.) *homework*
decir *to say, tell*
dejar *to leave*
de nada *you're welcome*
delgado *thin*
dentro *within, inside*
dependiente/a *shop assistant*
deporte (m.) *sport*
derecha: a la — *on the right*
desayunar *to have breakfast*
descansar *to rest*
desde *from*
degraciadamente *unfortunately*
despacho (m.) *study, office*

despertar *to wake up*
después *afterwards*
día (m.) *day*
difícil *difficult*
dinero (m.) *money*
dirección (f.) *address*; en — a *towards*
disponer de *to have*
distancia (f.) *distance*
distinto *different*
doblar *to turn*
doble *double*
domingo *Sunday*
dormir *to sleep*
ducharse *to shower*
dudar *to doubt*
durante *during*

echar una carta *to post a letter*
edificio (m.) *building*
ejemplo (m.) *example*
encantar *to like, love*
encontrar *to find*
encontrarse *to meet, be, be situated*
enfadarse *to get annoyed*
enfermarse *to become ill*
enfrente *opposite*
ensalada (f.) *salad*
enseñar *to teach*
entonces *then*
entrada (f.) *entrance*
entrevistarse *to have talks*
enviar *to send*
equipaje (m.) *luggage*
escocés *Scottish*
escritorio (m.) *desk*
escuchar *to listen*
escuela (f.) *school*
esfuerzo (m.) *effort*
espacio (m.) *space*
español *Spanish*
esperar *to wait, hope, expect*
esquiar *to ski*
esquina (f.) *corner*
estación (f.) *station*; — de servicio *service station*
estar *to be*
estrella (f.) *star*
estudiante (m./f.) *student*
estudiar *to study*
estupendo *great, fantastic*
exigir *to demand*
existir *to exist*
éxito (m.) *success*

expedir *to despatch*
exterior *facing the street*
extranjero *foreign*; (m.) *foreigner*

fábrica (f.) *factory*
fabricar *to manufacture*
fácil *easy*
factura (f.) *invoice, bill*
falda (f.) *skirt*
faltar *to miss, be absent*
familia (f.) *family*
farmacia (f.) *chemist's*
fecha (f.) *date*
feliz *happy*
fijo *fixed*
final: al — de *at the end of*
finales: a — de *at the end of*
fin de semana (m.) *weekend*
fino *good*
firma (f.) *firm, company*
formulario (m.) *form*
fotografía (f.) *photograph*
freír *to fry*
frío *cold*
frito *fried*
fruta (f.) *fruit*
fuego (m.) *light*
fuera *out, outside*
fumar *to smoke*

gafas (f. pl.) *glasses*
galleta (f.) *biscuit*
ganar *to earn*
gasolinera (f.) *petrol station*
gente (f.) *people*
gerente (m./f.) *manager*
girar *to turn*
gobierno (m.) *government*
gordo *fat*
gótico *gothic*
gracias *thank you*
gran *big, large, great*
grande *big, large*
guapo *good looking, pretty*
guía (m./f.) *guide (person)*
gustar *to like*

habitación (f.) *room*
hablar *to speak*
hacer *to do, make*
hacer falta *to need*
hallarse *to be situated*
hambre (f.) *hunger*
hasta *until, as far as*

hay que *one has to*
hermano (m.) *brother*
hijo/a *son/daughter*
hindú *Indian*
hola *hello*
hombre (m.) *man*
hora (f.) *hour*; a la — *on time*
horario de trabajo (m.) *working
  hours*
húmedo *wet* (climate)

iglesia (f.) *church*
imaginar *to imagine*
importar *to mind*
indicar *to indicate*
individual *single*
inglés *English*
iniciar *to start, begin*
inmediato: de — *right away*
instalar *to install, establish*
instituto (m.) *school*
interesar *to interest*
interior *at the back*
invitado/a *guest*; — de honor
  guest of honour
irlandés *Irish*
irse *to leave*
izquierda: a la — *on the left*
jardín (m.) *garden*
jefe/a *manager, boss, head*
jefe/a de gobierno *head of
  government*
jefe/a de ventas *sales manager*
jugar *to play*
juntos *together*

lado: al — de *next to*
lana (f.) *wool*
largo *long*
lástima (f.) *pity*
lavarse *to wash oneself*
leer *to read*
lejos *far*
levantar *to lift*
levantarse *to get up*
libre *free*
libro (m.) *book*
limpio *clean*
listo *ready*
luego *then*
lugar (m.) *place*
lunes *Monday*
luz (f.) *light*
llamada (f.) *call*
llamar *to call*

llamarse *to be called*
llave (f.) *key*
llegar *to arrive*
llevar *to carry*; — + gerund *to
  have been doing something*
llover *to rain*
lluvia (f.) *rain*

madera (f.) *wood*
maleta (f.) *suitcase*
maletín (m.) *small suitcase*
malo *bad*
manzana (f.) *block; apple*
manera: de — que *so that*; de esta
  — *in this way*
mano (f.) *hand*
mañana *tomorrow*; (f.) *morning*
marcharse *to leave*
marido (m.) *husband*
marrón *brown*
más *more, else*
más o menos *more or less*
material de oficina (m.) *office
  material*
mayor *elderly*
medicina (f.) *medicine*
médico/a *doctor*
mediodía (m.) *midday*
mejor *better*; a lo — *perhaps*
mentira (f.) *lie*
menudo: a — *often*
mercado (m.) *market*
mes (m.) *month*
mesa (f.) *table*
mexicano *Mexican*
mientras *while, whilst*
ministro/a *minister*
minuto (m.) *minute*
molestarse *to be annoyed*
moneda (f.) *currency*
moreno *tanned*
morir *to die*
motivo (m.) *reason*
muchacho/a *boy/girl*
mucho *much, a lot*; — gusto
  pleased to meet you
muerto *dead*
mujer (f.) *woman, wife*
museo (m.) *museum*
muy *very*

nacer *to be born*
nada *nothing*
nadar *to swim*
nadie *nobody*

naranja (f.) *orange*
Navidades (f. pl.) *Christmas*
necesitar *to need*
ninguno *none, any*
niño/a *child*
noche (f.) *night*
normalmente *normally*
norte (m.) *north*
noticia (f.) *news*
nuevamente *again*
nuevo *new*
número (m.) *number*

obligar *to force*
obtener *to obtain*
ocupado *busy*
ocupar *to occupy*
ocurrir *to happen*
oferta (f.) *offer*; de — *special offer*
oficina (f.) *office*
oficio (m.) *trade*
oír *to hear*
ojo (m.) *eye*
opinar *to think*
orden (m.) *order, kind*
ordenador (m.) *computer*
ordenar *to order*
oro (m.) *gold*
otra vez *again*
otro *other, another*

pagar *to pay*
país (m.) *country*
pan (m.) *bread*
panadería (f.) *baker's*
pantalones (m. pl.) *trousers*
papelería (f.) *stationer's*
paquete (m.) *parcel, package*
par (m.) *pair*
para *for, in order to*
parecer *to seem*
pariente (m.) *relative*
pasado *last, past*; — mañana *the day after tomorrow*
pasar *to come in, come by, spend (time), to pass*
pasarlo bien *to have a good time*
paseo (m.) *walk*
película (f.) *film*
peluquería (f.) *hairdresser's*
pensar *to think*
perdonar *to forgive*
perdone *excuse me*
periódico (m.) *newspaper*

permiso de trabajo (m.) *work permit*
perro (m.) *dog*
persona (f.) *person*
personalmente *personally*
pertenecer *to belong*
peruano *Peruvian*
pescado (m.) *fish*
piscina (f.) *swimming pool*
piso (m.) *flat*
plancha: a la — *grilled*
playa (f.) *beach*
pobre *poor*
poco *little*
poder *to be able to, can*
pollo (m.) *chicken*
poner *to put*
por *for, by, per, at*; — aquí *this way*
por favor *please*
por supuesto *certainly*
portero (m.) *porter*
precio (m.) *price*
precioso *beautiful*
preguntar *to ask*
preocupado *worried*
preocuparse *to worry*
preparar *to prepare*
presentar *to introduce*
primero *first*
primo/a *cousin*
príncipe (m.) *prince*
privado *private*
probarse *to try on*
problema (m.) *problem*
producir *to produce*
profesor/a *teacher*
propiedad (f.) *property*
propio *own*
próximo *next*
publicar *to publish*
pueblo (m.) *town, village*
puerta (f.) *door*
puerto (m.) *port*
pues *well, then, because*
qué *what, which*; ¿— tal? *how are you?*
quedarse *to stay*
quejarse *to complain*
querer *to want, love*
quién *who*
quitarse *to take off* (clothes)
quizá *perhaps*

raro *strange*

rato (m.) *while, moment*
razón (f.) *reason;* tener — *to be right*
recado (m.) *message*
recibir *to receive*
recoger *to pick up*
recto *straight;* todo — *straight on*
redondo *round*
regresar *to return*
reiterar *to reiterate*
rellenar *to fill in*
reparar *to repair*
reserva (f.) *reservation*
resfriado: estar — *to have a cold*
reunión (f.) *meeting*
revista (f.) *magazine*
rico *rich*
robo (m.) *theft*
rojo *red*
ruido (m.) *noise*
ruidoso *noisy*

sábado *Saturday*
saber *to know, know how to*
sabroso *tasty*
sacar *to get, buy* (tickets), *take out*
sal (f.) *salt*
saludar *to greet*
secretario/a *secretary*
seguir *to follow, continue*
segundo *second*
seguro: estar — *to be sure; sure, certain*
semáforo (m.) *traffic light*
semana (f.) *week*
sentir *to be sorry*
señor (m.) *Mr, sir, gentleman*
señora (f.) *Mrs, madam, lady*
señorita (f.) *Miss, young lady*
ser *to be*
servicios (m. pl.) *toilets*
siempre *always*
sierra (f.) *mountain*
simpático *nice*
solamente *only*
soler *to be in the habit of, to usually*
solicitar *to request*
solicitud (f.) *application form*
solo *alone*
sólo *only*
soltero *single*
sonar *to ring*

sopa de verduras (f.) *vegetable soup*
sostener *to hold*
suceder *to happen*
sucio *dirty*
supermercado (m.) *supermarket*
supuesto: por — *of course, certainly*

talla (f.) *size* (clothes)
tal vez *perhaps*
tamaño (m.) *size*
también *also*
tarde *late;* buenas tardes *good afternoon/evening*
té (m.) *tea*
teatro (m.) *theatre*
televisor (m.) *television set*
tema (m.) *subject*
temer *to fear*
templado *temperate*
temprano *early*
tener *to have;* — que *to have to*
terminar *to finish*
tiempo (m.) *time*
tienda (f.) *shop*
Tierra (f.) *Earth*
tímido *shy*
tinto *red* (wine)
tío/a *uncle/aunt*
tirar *to throw away*
tocar *to play* (an instrument)
todavía *still, yet*
todo *everything;* — recto *straight on*
todos *all*
tomar notas *to take notes*
tono de marcar (m.) *dialling tone*
tonto/a *fool*
trabajar *to work*
traer *to bring*
tráfico (m.) *traffic*
tranquilidad (f.) *peace*
tranquilo *quiet, relaxed*
trasladar *to take, transfer*
tratar *to deal with*
tren (m.) *train*
triste *sad*
trono (m.) *throne*
trozo (m.) *piece*

última vez *last time*
último *last*
universidad (f.) *university*

unos *some, about*

vacaciones (f. pl.) *holiday*
vale *OK*
valer *to cost*
vamos *let's go*
vender *to sell*
ventana (f.) *window*
ver *to see*
verano (m.) *summer*
verdad (f.) *truth*
verde *green*
vestido (m.) *dress*
vez (f.) *time*; de — en cuando
  from time to time; otra —
  again; una — *once*; a veces
  sometimes

viajar *to travel*
viaje (m.) *trip, journey, travel*; —
  de negocios *business trip*
viajero/a *traveller*
viento (m.) *wind*; hace — *it's
  windy*
vino (m.) *wine*
visado (m.) *visa*
visita (f.) *visit*
vista (f.) *view*
volver *to return, come back*

ya *already*

zapatería (f.) *shoe shop*
zapato (m.) *shoe*
zumo (m.) *juice*

English–Spanish vocabulary

able (to be – to) *poder*
accept (to) *aceptar*
accompany (to) *acompañar*
address *dirección* (f.)
aeroplane *avión* (m.)
after *después*
afterwards *después*
again *otra vez, nuevamente*
agency *agencia* (f.)
airport *aeropuerto* (m.)
all *todo(s)/a(s)*
all right *de acuerdo*
alone *solo/a*
also *también*
although *aunque*
always *siempre*
Andalusian *andaluz/a*
annoyed (to be) *estar enfadado/a*
annoyed (to get) *enfadarse,
  molestarse*
annoyed *enfadado/a*
another *otro/a*
any *alguno/a(s)*
any (not) *ninguno/a*
anybody *alguien*
anything *algo*
apartment *apartamento* (m.)
apple *manzana* (f.)
application form *solicitud* (f.)
appointment *cita* (f.)
approach (to) *acercarse*
Argentinian *argentino/a*
arrive (to) *llegar*
art *arte* (f.)
article *artículo* (m.)
as far as *hasta*

as soon as possible *lo antes
  posible*
ask (to) *preguntar*
at *en*
attend (to) *asistir*
aunt *tía* (f.)
authority *autoridad* (f.)
autumn *otoño* (m.)

bad *malo/a*
bag *bolso* (m.)
baker's *panadería* (f.)
ballpoint pen *bolígrafo* (m.)
bank *banco* (m.)
bathroom *baño* (m.)
be (to) *ser, estar*
be glad (to) *alegrarse*
be in the habit of (to) *acostumbrar*
beach *playa* (f.)
beautiful *bonito/a, precioso/a*
because *porque*
bed *cama* (f.)
before *antes*
begin (to) *empezar, comenzar*
belong (to) *pertenecer*
besides *además*
better *mejor*
bicycle *bicicleta* (f.)
big *grande*
bill *cuenta* (f.); *factura* (f.)
  (invoice)
birthday *cumpleaños* (m.)
biscuit *galleta* (f.)
black *negro/a*
block *manzana* (f.); *cuadra* (f.)
  (L. Am.)

blouse   *blusa* (f.)
blue   *azul*
book   *libro* (m.)
boring   *aburrido/a*
born (to be)   *nacer*
boss   *jefe/a*
bottle   *botella* (f.)
boy   *niño, muchacho, chico* (m.)
bread   *pan* (m.)
breakfast (to have)   *desayunar*
breakfast   *desayuno* (m.)
bring (to)   *traer*
British   *británico/a*
brother   *hermano*
brown   *marrón*
building   *edificio* (m.)
business   *negocio* (m.)
busy   *ocupado/a*
butcher's   *carnicería* (f.)
buy (to)   *comprar*
by   *por*

call (to)   *llamar*
call   *llamada* (f.)
called (to be)   *llamarse*
can   *poder (to be able to)*
car park   *aparcamiento* (m.),
   estacionamiento (Southern Cone,
   L. Am.)
car   *coche* (m.); *carro* (m.), *auto*
   (m.) (L. Am.)
carry (to)   *llevar*
case   *caja* (f.)
case (in that)   *en ese caso*
cash point   *cajero automático* (m.)
catch (to)   *coger*
cathedral   *catedral* (f.)
Catholic   *católico/a*
centre   *centro* (m.)
certainly   *por supuesto*
change (to)   *cambiar*
change   *cambio* (m.)
cheap   *barato/a*
chemist's   *farmacia* (f.)
chicken   *pollo* (m.)
Chilean   *chileno/a*
Christmas   *Navidad (f, sing)*,
   Navidades (f, pl)
church   *iglesia* (f.)
cinema   *cine* (m.)
city   *ciudad* (f.)
clean   *limpio/a*
climate   *clima* (m.)
cold (it is–)   *hace frío*
cold   *frío/a*

colour   *color* (m.)
come (to)   *venir*
come back (to)   *volver, regresar*
come in (to)   *pasar, entrar*
comfortable   *cómodo/a*
company   *compañía* (f.), *empresa*
   (f.), *firma* (f.)
complain (to)   *quejarse*
computer   *ordenador* (m.);
   computadora (f.) (L. Am.)
consider (to)   *considerar; pensar*
continue (to)   *continuar, seguir*
cook (to)   *cocinar*
corner   *esquina* (f.); *rincón* (m.)
cost (to)   *valer, costar*
country   *país* (m.); *campo* (m.)
countryside   *campo* (m.)
course   *curso* (m.)
cousin   *primo/a*
cross (to)   *cruzar*
currency   *moneda* (f.)
current account   *cuenta corriente*
   (f.)
cut (to)   *cortar*

dance (to)   *bailar*
date   *fecha* (f.)
daughter   *hija* (f.)
day after tomorrow (the)   *pasado*
   mañana
day before yesterday (the) *anteayer*,
   antes de ayer, antier (Mexico)
day   *día* (m.)
dead   *muerto/a*
deal with (to)   *tratar*
demand (to)   *exigir*
desk   *escritorio* (m.)
despatch (to)   *despachar, enviar,*
   expedir
dialling tone   *tono de marcar* (m.)
die (to)   *morir*
different   *diferente, distinto/a*
difficult   *difícil*
dining room   *comedor* (m.)
dinner   *cena* (f.)
dirty   *sucio/a*
distance   *distancia* (f.)
district   *barrio* (m.)
do (to)   *hacer*
doctor   *médico/a, doctor/a*
dog   *perro/a*
door   *puerta* (f.)
double   *doble*
doubt (to)   *dudar*
downstairs   *abajo*

dress   *vestido* (m.)
drink (to)   *beber; tomar* (L. Am.)
drink   *copa* (f.); *bebida* (f.)
drive (to)   *conducir*
during   *durante*
dusk   *atardecer* (m.)

each   *cada*
early   *temprano, pronto*
earn (to)   *ganar*
Earth   *Tierra* (f.)
easy   *fácil*
eat (to)   *comer*
effort   *esfuerzo* (m.)
eighth   *octavo/a*
elderly   *mayor*
else   *más*
end (at the – of)   *al final de
   (location); a finales de (time)*
English   *inglés/inglesa; inglés* (m.)
   (language)
enough   *bastante, suficiente*
entrance   *entrada* (f.)
establish (to)   *instalar, establecer*
evening   *atardecer* (m.)
ever   *alguna vez*
every   *todos/as*
everything   *todo*
example   *ejemplo* (m.)
excuse (to)   *perdonar*
exist (to –)   *existir*
expect (to)   *esperar*
expensive   *caro/a*
eye   *ojo* (m.)

factory   *fábrica* (f.)
fall (to)   *caer*
family   *familia* (f.)
far   *lejos*
farmer   *campesino/a*
fat   *gordo/a*
father   *padre* (m.)
fear (to)   *temer*
fetch   *(to)* buscar
fifth   *quinto/a*
fill in (to)   *rellenar*
film   *película* (f.)
find (to)   *encontrar*
finish (to)   *terminar*
firm   *firma* (f.), *empresa* (f.),
   compañía (f.)
first   *primero/a*
fish   *pescado* (m.)
fixed   *fijo/a*
flat   *piso* (m.), *apartamento* (m.)

follow (to)   *seguir*
food   *comida* (f.), *alimento* (m.)
fool   *tonto/a*
for   *por, para*
force (to)   *obligar*
foreign   *extranjero/a*
foreigner   *extranjero/a*
forgive (to)   *perdonar*
form   *formulario* (m.)
fourth   *cuarto/a*
free   *libre*
Friday   *viernes* (m.)
fried   *frito/a*
friend   *amigo/a*
from time to time   *de vez en
   cuando*
from   *de, desde*
fruit   *fruta* (f.)
fry (to)   *freír*

garden   *jardín* (m.)
gentleman   *señor* (m.)
get (to)   *conseguir*
get up (to)   *levantarse*
girl   *niña, muchacha, chica* (f.)
give (to)   *dar*
glasses   *gafas (f, pl)*
go down (to)   *bajar*
go to bed (to)   *acostarse*
gold   *oro* (m.)
good afternoon   *buenas tardes*
good evening   *buenas tardes,
   buenas noches*
good looking   *guapo/a*
good morning   *buenos días*
good night   *buenas noches*
good   *bueno/a; fino/a*
government   *gobierno* (m.)
grandfather   *abuelo*
grandmother   *abuela*
grandparents   *abuelos (m, pl)*
great   *estupendo/a (fantastic); gran
   (important)*
green   *verde*
greet (to)   *saludar*
grilled   *a la plancha*
guest   *invitado/a*
guide   *guía (m/f) (person); guía* (f.)
   (book)

hairdresser's   *peluquería* (f.)
hand   *mano* (f.)
handbag   *bolso* (m.)
happen (to)   *ocurrir, suceder, pasar*
happy   *feliz, contento/a*

have (to – to) *tener que, deber*
have (to) *tener, contar con,*
  disponer de
have a cold (to) *estar resfriado,*
  estar constipado (Spain)
have just (to) *acabar de*
have lunch (to) *almorzar*
head of government *jefe/a de*
  gobierno
head *cabeza* (f.)
hear (to) *oír*
heat *calor* (m.)
hello *hola*
help (to) *ayudar*
help *ayuda* (f.)
here *aquí*
highway *carretera* (f.)
hire (to) *contratar (a person);*
  alquilar (a house, a car)
hold (to) *sostener*
holiday *vacaciones (f, pl)*
homework *deberes (m, pl)*
hope (to) *esperar*
hot *caliente, caluroso (weather)*
hour *hora*
house *casa* (f.)
how are you? *¿qué tal?, ¿cómo*
  está(s)?
how many *cuántos/as*
how much *cuánto/a*
how *cómo*
hunger *hambre* (f.)
husband *marido, esposo* (m.)

ill (to become) *enfermarse*
imagine (to) *imaginar*
in *en*
Indian *indio/a, hindú*
indicate (to) *indicar*
inside *dentro*
install (to) *instalar, establecer*
interest (to) *interesar*
introduce (to) *presentar*
invoice *factura* (f.)
Irish *irlandés/irlandesa*

jacket *chaqueta* (f.)
journey *viaje* (m.)
juice *zumo; jugo (L. Am.)*

key *llave* (f.)
kind *amable*
kitchen *cocina* (f.)
know (to) *conocer, saber*
know how to (to) *saber*

lady *señora, señorita* (f.)
large *grande*
last year *año pasado* (m.)
last *pasado/a; último/a*
late *tarde*
lawyer *abogado/a*
learn (to) *aprender*
leave (to) *irse, marcharse, dejar*
left (on the) *a la izquierda*
left *izquierdo/a*
letter *carta* (f.)
library *biblioteca* (f.)
lie *mentira* (f.)
lift (to) *levantar*
light *fuego* (m.); *luz* (f.)
like (to) *gustar*
like *como*
listen (to) *escuchar*
little *poco/a (amount); pequeño/a*
  (size)
long *largo/a*
look after (to) *cuidar, atender*
look for (to) *buscar*
lot (a) *mucho/a*
love (to) *gustar mucho, encantar*
luggage *equipaje* (m.)
lunch *almuerzo* (m.), *comida* (f.)

madam *señora*
magazine *revista* (f.)
mail *correspondencia* (f.)
make (to) *hacer*
man *hombre*
manager *gerente, jefe/a*
morning *mañana* (f.)
manufacture (to) *fabricar*
market *mercado* (m.)
married *casado/a*
meat *carne* (f.)
medicine *medicina* (f.)
meet (to) *encontrarse; conocer (to*
  get to know)
meeting *reunión* (f.)
menu *menú* (m.), *carta* (f.)
message *recado* (m.), *mensaje* (m.)
Mexican *mexicano/a*
midday *mediodía* (m.)
mind (to) *importar*
minister *ministro/a*
minute *minuto* (m.)
miss (to) *faltar (to be absent);*
  perder (transport); echar de
  menos/extrañar (L. Am.)
  (nostalgia)

Miss *señorita*
moment *momento* (m.), *rato* (m.)
Monday *lunes* (m.)
money *dinero* (m.)
month *mes* (m.)
more or less *más o menos*
more *más*
mother *madre*
mountain *montaña* (f.), *sierra* (f.)
Mr *señor*
Mrs *señora*
much *mucho/a*
museum *museo* (m.)
must *deber, tener que*

near *cerca*
need (to) *necesitar, hacer falta*
never *nunca, jamás*
New Year *Año Nuevo* (m.)
new *nuevo/a*
news *noticia* (f.)
newspaper *periódico* (m.), *diario* (m.)
next to *al lado de*
next *próximo/a*
nice *bonito/a; simpático/a (person)*
night *noche* (f.)
ninth *noveno/a*
nobody *nadie*
noise *ruido* (m.)
noisy *ruidoso/a*
none *ninguno/a*
normally *normalmente*
north *norte* (m.)
nothing *nada*
now *ahora*
number *número* (m.)

obtain (to) *obtener*
occupy (to) *ocupar*
of course *por supuesto*
of *de*
offer *oferta* (f.)
offer (special) *de oferta*
office *oficina* (f.), *despacho* (m.)
often *a menudo*
OK *vale (especially Spain)*
on *en*
once *una vez*
onion *cebolla* (f.)
only *sólo, solamente*
opposite *enfrente*
orange *naranja* (f.) *(fruit)*; *naranja* *(m/f) (colour)*
order (in – to) *para*

order (to) *ordenar*
order *orden* (m.)
others *otros/as*
out *fuera*
outside *fuera*
own *propio/a*

package *paquete* (m.)
pair *par* (m.)
parcel *paquete* (m.)
park (to) *aparcar, estacionar* *(Southern Cone, L. Am.)*
past *pasado/a*
pay (to –) *pagar*
peace *tranquilidad* (f.)
people *gente (f, sing)*
per *por*
perhaps *a lo mejor, tal vez, quizá(s)*
persona *person* (f.)
personally *personalmente*
Peruvian *peruano/a*
petrol station *gasolinera* (f.)
photograph *foto* (f.), *fotografía* (f.)
pick up (to) *recoger*
piece *trozo* (m.)
pity *lástima* (f.)
place *lugar* (m.), *sitio* (m.)
play (to) *jugar; tocar (an instrument)*
please *por favor*
pleased to meet you *mucho gusto, encantado/a*
polluted *contaminado/a*
poor *pobre*
pork chop *chuleta de cerdo* (f.)
pork *cerdo* (m.)
port *puerto* (m.)
porter *portero/a*
post office *(oficina de) correos* (f.)
post *(to – a letter)* *echar una carta*
prepare (to) *preparar*
pretty *bonito/a*
price *precio* (m.)
prince *príncipe* (m.)
private *privado*
problem *problema* (m.)
produce (to) *producir*
property *propiedad* (f.)
publish (to) *publicar*
put (to) *poner*

question *pregunta* (f.)

quiet   *tranquilo/a*
quite   *bastante*

rain   *lluvia* (f.)
rain (to)   *llover*
read (to)   *leer*
ready   *listo/a*
reason   *motivo* (m.), *razón* (f.)
receive (to)   *recibir*
receiver   *auricular* (m.)
red   *rojo/a; tinto (wine)*
relative   *pariente (m/f)*
rent (to)   *alquilar*
rent   *alquiler* (m.)
repair (to)   *reparar*
request (to)   *solicitar*
reservation   *reserva* (f.);
    reservación (f.) (L. Am.)
rest (to)   *descansar*
return   *(to) regresar, volver;*
    devolver (something)
rich   *rico/a*
right (on the)   *a la derecha*
right (to be)   *tener razón*
right away   *de inmediato, ahora*
    mismo
right now   *ahora mismo*
right   *derecho/a*
ring (to)   *sonar*
room   *habitación* (f.), *cuarto* (m.)
round   *redondo/a*

sad   *triste*
salad   *ensalada* (f.)
sales manager   *jefe/a de ventas*
salt   *sal* (f.)
Saturday   *sábado* (m.)
say (to –)   *decir*
school   *colegio* (m.), *escuela* (f.);
    instituto (m.) (secondary school,
    Spain)
Scottish   *escocés/escocesa*
second   *segundo/a*
secretary   *secretario/a*
see (to)   *ver*
seem (to)   *parecer*
sell (to)   *vender*
send (to)   *enviar, mandar*
seventh   *séptimo/a*
share (to)   *compartir*
shirt   *camisa* (f.)
shoe shop   *zapatería* (f.)
shoe   *zapato* (m.)
shop assistant   *dependiente/a*
shop   *tienda* (f.)

short   *bajo/a*
shower (to)   *ducharse*
shower   *ducha* (f.)
shy   *tímido/a*
single   *soltero/a (marital status);*
    individual (room)
sir   *señor*
sister   *hermana* (f.)
situated (to be)   *estar situado/a,*
    encontrarse, hallarse
sixth   *sexto/a*
size   *tamaño* (m.) (volume); *talla*
    (f.) (clothing)
ski (to)   *esquiar*
skirt   *falda* (f.)
sleep (to)   *dormir*
smoke (to)   *fumar*
so that   *de manera que*
some   *unos/as, algunos/as*
somebody   *alguien*
something   *algo*
sometimes   *a veces*
son   *hijo* (m.)
soup   *sopa* (f.)
south   *sur* (m.)
space   *espacio* (m.)
Spanish   *español/a; español* (m.)
    (language)
speak (to)   *hablar*
spend (to)   *pasar (time); gastar*
    (money)
sport   *deporte* (m.)
sports centre   *centro deportivo* (m.)
spring   *primavera* (f.)
star   *estrella* (f.)
start (to)   *empezar, comenzar*
station (service)   *estación de*
    servicio (f.), *gasolinera* (f.)
station   *estación* (f.)
stationer's   *papelería* (f.)
stay (to)   *quedarse*
still   *todavía*
straight on   *todo recto*
strange   *raro/a*
street   *calle* (f.)
student   *estudiante*
study (to)   *estudiar*
study   *despacho* (m.)
subject   *tema* (m.) (topic)
success   *éxito* (m.)
suitcase   *maleta* (f.)
summer   *verano* (m.)
Sunday   *domingo* (m.)
sunglasses   *gafas de sol (f, pl)*
supermarket   *supermercado* (m.)

sure (to be) *estar seguro*
swim (to) *nadar*
swimming pool *piscina* (f.);
  alberca (f.) (Mexico)

table *mesa* (f.)
tablet *comprimido* (m.), *tableta*
  (f.), *pastilla* (f.)
take (to) *tomar, coger*
take off (to) *quitarse (clothes)*;
  despegar (aeroplane)
talks (to have) *entrevistarse*
talks *conversaciones (f, pl)*
tall *alto/a*
tanned *moreno/a*
tasty *sabroso/a*
tea *té* (m.)
teach (to) *enseñar*
teacher *profesor/a, maestro/a*
television *televisión* (f.)
tell (to) *decir, contar*
temperate *templado/a*
tenth *décimo/a*
thank you *gracias*
that *ese/esa (demonstrative); que
  (relative pronoun)*
theatre *teatro* (m.)
theft *robo* (m.)
then *entonces; en seguida, después*
there is/are *hay*
there *allí*
thin *delgado/a*
think (to) *opinar; creer; pensar;
  considerar*
third *tercero/a*
throw away (to) *tirar*
Thursday *jueves* (m.)
ticket *billete* (m.), *boleto* (m.)
  (L. Am.)
tie *corbata* (f.)
time (last –) *última vez*
time (on –) *a la hora*
time (to have a good –) *pasarlo
  bien*
time *tiempo* (m.)
today *hoy*
together *juntos/as*
toilet *lavabo* (m.), *servicios (m, pl)*
tomorrow *mañana*
towards *en dirección a*
town hall *ayuntamiento* (m.)
town *ciudad* (f.), *pueblo* (m.)
trade *oficio* (m.)
traffic light *semáforo* (m.)
traffic *tráfico* (m.)

train *tren* (m.)
travel (to) *viajar*
travel agency *agencia de viajes* (f.)
traveller *viajero/a*
trip *viaje* (m.)
trousers *pantalón (m, sing),
  pantalones (m, pl)*
truth *verdad* (f.)
try (to – on) *probarse*
Tuesday *martes* (m.)
turn (to) *girar, doblar*
twice *dos veces*

uncle *tío* (m.)
unfortunately *desgraciadamente,
  desafortunadamente*
university *universidad* (f.)
until *hasta*
upstairs *arriba*
usually *generalmente,
  normalmente*

vegetable *verdura* (f.)
very *muy*
view *vista* (f.)
village *pueblo* (m.)
visa *visado* (m.), *visa* (f.) (L. Am.)
visit *visita* (f.)

wait (to) *esperar*
waiter *camarero, mesero* (L. Am.)
waitress *camarera, mesera* (L. Am.)
wake (to – up) *despertar (se)*
walk *paseo* (m.)
walk (to) *andar, caminar*
want (to) *querer*
warm (it is –) *hace calor*
wash (to – oneself) *lavarse*
watch (to) *mirar, ver*
way (in this) *de esta manera*
way (this) *por aquí*
way *camino* (m.); *manera* (f.),
  modo (m.)
Wednesday *miércoles* (m.)
week *semana* (f.)
weekend *fin de semana* (m.)
welcome (you´re –) *de nada, no
  hay de qué*
well *bien*
wet *húmedo/a (climate)*
what *qué, cuál/cuáles (sing/pl)*
which *cuál/cuáles (sing/pl)*
while *mientras; rato* (m.)
whilst *mientras*
white *blanco/a*

who *quien/quienes*
why? *¿por qué?*
wife *mujer, esposa* (f.)
wind *viento* (m.)
window *ventana* (f.)
wine *vino* (m.)
winter *invierno* (m.)
with me/you *conmigo/contigo (familiar)/con usted (formal)*
with *con*
within *dentro*
woman *mujer* (f.)
wood *madera* (f.)
wool *lana* (f.)

work (to) *trabajar*
work permit *permiso de trabajo* (m.)
working hours *horario de trabajo* (m.)
worried *preocupado/a*
worry (to) *preocuparse*
worse *peor*

year *año* (m.)
yellow *amarillo/a*
yesterday *ayer*
yet *todavía*